30 Days of Gratitude

30 Days of Gratitude

Use Your Words to Change Your Life.

SOPHIA MATTIS, MD, MHSA

I AM Ignites

New York

30 Days of Gratitude: Use Your Words to Change Your Life by Dr. Sophia Mattis

Published by I Am Ignites
209 Glen Cove Rd. Suite 508
Carle Place, NY 11514

The author has made every attempt to note accurate Internet addresses during the time of publication, neither the author nor publisher assume any liability for errors or changes occurring after the publication of the book.

ISBN: 978-1-7344795-2-2

Library of Congress Control Number: Pending

Printed in the United States of America

Dedication

I dedicate this book to the One who is *the* only true source, my source of everything, Abba. Father, I love You.

To every soul who thinks it's impossible to *merely* give thanks without asking for anything.

"And therefore will the LORD wait, that he may be gracious unto you,

and therefore will he be exalted, that he may have mercy upon you:

for the LORD is a God of judgment: blessed are all they that wait for him."

~ Isaiah 30:18 ~

Contents

Acknowledgments

To the ones who love me most, dad Errol and mama Winnie. Thank you for accepting me for who I am and understanding who I was born to be.

Indeed, it snows in H.C., but there's no snow in Panama, Jamaica, Freeport nor Belize. A prophet, a pastor, an apostle to be, your reading and writing make things plainer to see. While Death Valley sends her scorching heat, that one, not this one, makes her way from the south just to see me.

Introduction

Have you ever heard GOD say, "No more asking for things?" How about hearing GOD say, "For the next 30 days I don't want you to ask for anything. For the next 30 days, only express appreciation. For the next 30 days don't ask Me for a anything. Instead, just be grateful."

Gratitude is paramount!

This book will season you to pray with gratitude while offering up praise. With each day you spend giving gratitude and penning the things you are thankful for; you'll begin to develop a habitual gratitude-filled prayer life. Most of all, I pray that once you've completed this 30-day journey of gratitude, you'll be conditioned to:

"Enter into His gate with thanksgiving, and into His court with praise: be thankful unto Him, and bless His name."

- The Holy Bible

Psalm 100:4 (KJV)

Sophia Mattis

30 Days of Gratitude

"I will praise thee, O LORD, with my whole heart; I will shew forth all thy marvellous works."

~ Psalm 9:1 ~

A 30-Day Journey

There's a popular saying among the Christian community that goes like this, "As the prayers go up, the blessings come down." I believe this saying and so should you! Praise GOD in *all* situations and in *all* things and watch how GOD transforms your life. Watch how you become a more peaceful and joyful person.

I wondered what it would be like to *never* ask GOD for a thing. If you're anything like me, even just a smidgen like me, you'd be wondering the same thing. You may even be asking yourself, "I wonder how I'm going to do this "not asking" for anything?" At first glance, it may seem scary or even unattainable, but when you sit and ponder, you begin feeling a glimpse of hope. Once the initial shock subsides, you begin feeling as if the task is achievable. I know for me, I thought I would've been turning blue! I thought I would've felt as if someone just knocked the wind out of me. I thought I would've been feeling like someone sucker punched me! Frankly, I thought I'd be mortified at even *thinking* about how to do such a thing. Well silly me. When GOD tells you to do something, then of course it's doable, period!

Days passed and I thought well, ok GOD, how about I start this gratitude thing on the 1st of August? Then I said, ok, I can start it now, but to chronicle this entire 30-day gratitude thing I think would be best done in about 2 weeks, during August! Hey, I thought August would be perfect! Afterall, it is my birthday month. How old am I you're wondering? Hum, let's see, if I was 25 last year, then this year that would make me 25!!! No, it's not a typo and don't go getting all cynical on me. I'm 25 every year! That's right, *25* every single solitary year, period, full stop! That's enough of that, let's get back on track.

August would've been the ideal month to start because: I would've been completely done with book # 2, it's my birthday month, and it's the beginning of a month which makes things easier, right? You know, day 1 would fall on the 1st day of the month and journaling would be easy to keep track of. Wrong! Although I thought that would've been the best thing ever, GOD said otherwise. Yup, He sure did and of course who always wins the battle, the war, the everything, GOD! So here I am on July 29th, 2020 at 4 a.m. starting this amazing journey of *30 Days of Gratitude*. How can I say it's amazing before I've even begun? Easy, what else feels better than being appreciated? Think about it. When someone expresses sincere appreciation toward you, you get all tingly inside. Well, don't you? I hope you do. You may even feel loved. When someone expresses gratitude toward you, you feel like doing more, not just for them, but for others. When someone expresses sincere gratitude toward you, your brain registers that as love and puts you in a happy space.

Truth be told, when GOD said, "30 days of gratitude," I paused and anticipated a some sort of strong fleshly reaction, but to my surprise, I got the exact opposite! During the moment I paused, my brain began rationalizing the entire request. My eyes started looking around, as they normally do when I'm wondering, GOD, is it really You? No, it's not because I'm not sure when GOD is speaking, but because I do that when I'm scheming on being disobedient. I'm not bragging here, just telling you the truth. Hey, don't judge me! When I hear the Father say something that seems challenging, I often sit and start saying things like GOD, is that You? In my asking, my eyes begin looking around as if GOD is going to appear. Well, I mean, technically, He could if He wanted to, right. So, when I don't want to do what the LORD has instructed me to do, the conversation between GOD and I goes something like this:

GOD: "30 Days of Gratitude. No asking for anything for the next 30 days."

Me: "GOD, is that You," with my eye's scanning the room.

GOD: Complete silence.

Then I hear crickets, the rustling of the wind, and everything except GOD.

Me: So, I repeat, "GOD, is that You?"

GOD: "30 Days of Gratitude."

Me: "GOD, is that really You?"

Now, this next part sometimes happens, but when it doesn't, it's the crickets I hear.

GOD: "Yes."

Me: "Jesus, is that You?"

GOD: "It's Me."

Me: "Me who?"

GOD: "Jesus."

Me: "Which Jesus? Jesus of Nazareth?"

Then, I hear nothing!

Yes, I know, it's comical, but right now some of you may be saying, "Well that's just disrespectful!" Guess what, stop it, because it's not! I have the *utmost* reverential fear of GOD. However, I also have a sense of humor, and might I remind you, GOD *gave me* this sense of humor! Stop thinking GOD is this rigid mean GOD! He is not! Yes, He is serious. However, He is also fun and loving. Beloved, when GOD instructs us to do something, please know it's for our benefit. GOD is GOD all by Himself and He doesn't need our help on *any* level. He chooses to do that which is: just, pure, lovely, and true. He chooses to help us be the best us even in the face of our sinful ways.

30 days. GOD said, "30 days." 30 days of gratitude and of course that's the name He gave me for this book. Yup, just that simple. I was a bit defiant because my

natural mind kept wondering, GOD, how am I supposed to finish *Epistles to Abba* and get it published before the 1st week of August if You have me starting *this* book? Well, I didn't get a reply, so that was that. About 1 week later, guess who began typing? You guessed right, that would be ME! No complaints here. I trust GOD, period. When the Father tells me to do something, I trust He knows best. I know He's already worked everything out for *my* good.

"The steps of a good man are ordered by the LORD: and he delighteth in his way." ~ Psalm 37:23

"For I know the thoughts that I think toward you, saith the LORD, thoughts of peace, and not of evil, to give you an expected end." ~ Jeremiah 29:11

"Looking unto Jesus the author and finisher of our *faith; who for the joy that was set before him endured the cross, despising the shame, and is set down at the right hand of the throne of God."* ~ Hebrews 12:2

As I type, I'm not certain of the structure of this book, but I am certain I will continue to type until my 30 days of gratitude is complete. For those of you who've read my previous books, you know my style is simple and relaxed. I don't believe in using words some people will stumble over neither do I believe in making a complex subject even more labyrinthian. Simple + funny + relaxed + relatable = digestible. See, even my math is simple. I expect you to be laughing at this point. Simply put, I've adopted one of my postgraduate instructor's philosophies, "Keep it simple stupid!" Sounds offensive, but truly, it is not. Fictional or not, there is no need to make storytelling herculean. Anyhow, I digress. Here's something I forgot to mention. After my initial pause when I heard the Father say, "Don't ask for anything for the next 30 days, I was pleasantly surprised to see how I was at total peace. Yes, believe it or not, I didn't go into a complete panic. Hysteria didn't set in, over the idea of not asking GOD for anything for one-whole-month! I thought, wow, ok GOD, 30 days of not asking for my usual? Hum. You know, the husband, the writing, the perfect fitness, the blah, blah,

blah. Hum, I said. Then I did my usual, you know, the upward gaze toward the ceiling, then my eyes darting off to the side, before I said, ok LORD, let's get it done! I know I said *let's get it done* as to include GOD when the request was given to me. Well of course I said, *let's*. You know, as in, let *us*. You must know by now that everything I do, I cannot, nor do I want to do it without GOD. It is only by the good and merciful grace of GOD that I get *anything* done at all. It is only by the good and merciful grace of GOD that *you* get anything done, whether you believe it or not. As for me, I already knew GOD Himself would help me. That's how wonderfully kind and magnificent our Abba GOD is, to say the least. Thank GOD He doesn't expect us to do things on our own! Hey, I'll even prove it to you right this second. When I received my instructions, I thought, ok, how am I going to go about doing this. Not to say I doubted the possibility of completing the task, but I wondered how can I assure I don't mess up? How can I *not* ask GOD for things during the next 30 days? Suddenly, I got a bright idea. NOT! Well, yes it was a bright idea, but the idea did not originate from me. It was Holy Spirit who planted the thought in my mind, as He does with all good thoughts.

A WOMAN GOES INTO A HOME IMPROVEMENT STORE AND SAYS TO AN EMPLOYEE, "PLEASE HELP ME TAKE THAT DO IT YOURSELF KIT OFF THE SHELF." THE EMPLOYEE SIGHS AND REPLIES, "IF I HELP YOU, THAT WILL DEFEAT THE PURPOSE?"

Jeremiah 9:23 says, *"Thus saith the LORD, Let not the wise man glory in his wisdom, neither let the mighty man glory in his might, let not the rich man glory in his riches:..."* So, what was the idea? I heard in my mind, "Everything you want to ask GOD for, turn it around." Meaning, be thankful for the very thing I want to ask GOD for. Brilliant! I mean, absolutely brilliant!!! Ok, so what does that mean? Let's say you want to ask GOD for His protection during your travels to and from work. Well instead of *asking* GOD for protection, simply *thank* GOD for His protection. Here's another example, let's say you want to be encouraged to make healthier eating choices, you can try saying something such as: "GOD, thank You for helping me to make healthy food choices or GOD thank You that I am making healthier meal choices. I believe you get the idea.

Below, I've listed a few common things many people ask GOD for. Below are some sample statements of how you can turn your *ask* around to your *thanks*. Let's move your desire from an ask to gratitude. Here goes.

Ask	*Gratitude*
1. GOD, please provide me with more money.	1. Thank You GOD for increased finances.
2. GOD, please help me exercise more.	2. GOD, thank You for helping me exercise today.
3. GOD, please heal me.	3. GOD, thank You for healing me.
4. GOD, give me joy.	4. GOD, thank You for giving me joy unspeakable.
5. GOD, please don't let there be any traffic.	5. GOD, thank You there's no traffic on my way home!

Criticism is avoidable only when you remain silent, remain still, and ascribe to be nothing.

For the next 30 days, you will journey with me as I give GOD all the glory, honor, and praise. You will witness how I give GOD complete gratitude for everything, how I thank GOD for things I'd love to ask for, and for the very things He's already given me. Even GOD's no, deserves a huge *thank you*, as His no is just as great as His yes. His no warrants just as much celebration as His yes! GOD's no is not to be seen as His denial, but instead, it ought to be seen as His glorious protection.

I believe wholeheartedly and feel comfortable saying I know you will have a wonderful transformation if you show sincere gratitude unto the Father. There is no higher form of praise unto the LORD than having an attitude of gratitude. Being grateful for who He is to you and overall, just being grateful for who He is period, is the attitude you should adopt. His majestic nature, His wondrous works, His omniscience, and all the gloriousness of His being is what you should celebrate. Despite your past, future, or your current situation, I assure you, GOD is great in *all* His ways.

Take this time to forget about all criticisms, past, present, and those to come. Place your focus on becoming a better you. I love this Aristotelian quote, the truth is, if you do nothing, if you say nothing, and as he says, be nothing, some people will still find something to criticize. One thing for sure is if you're doing nothing, some will criticize and say, "Look, they are doing nothing." The bottom line is, the world is full of critics frequently offering unsolicited criticism, whether constructive or not.

In this book, you will see 30 of my journals, 1 for each day, followed by a list of thank yous to the Father. Some of my thank yous are things already received, while others are things I am believing the LORD will bless me with. Now, as for you, follow the same format, utilizing a, journal your day and include your thank yous.

I've provided 4 blank pages for your journaling. Two pages are designated for journaling your day and prayer, one page is for listing your thank-yous, and the final page is for describing your feelings before, during, and/or after you wrote your thank yous. Take time to give each prayer some thought and be sure you're expressing sincere words during each exercise. Don't just go through the motions for the sake of getting something jotted down. Don't look at this exercise as a mere, checking the task off your bucket list. Remember, this is for *you* and *your* personal growth. Be honest. Write down your exact feelings before you started writing, while you're writing, and how you feel after you've completed your thought for that day. If you don't feel like praying, push beyond that feeling, and pray anyway, then record that feeling. If you didn't feel like praying, write that you didn't feel like praying. If you felt better after pushing beyond it, be sure you record that as well. If you're still apathetic, log that feeling too! The bottom line is, DON'T LIE! You're not taking a test and you don't have an audience. This is for *you* and you alone! This is for your spiritual growth and satisfaction. So above all else, please be honest.

As you think of the things you are thankful for, aim to list at least 5 or more points of gratitude. Remember to include things you want to ask the Father, but instead of asking, turn those things around to a thank you.

Finally, on day 31, take a moment to reflect and think about your month of gratitude. Reminisce on how you felt and things that occurred during your 30 days then go ahead and log those feelings and events. Log your *true* feelings. Go back and review each day's log and make note of any changes. Note all changes. This includes the good, the bad, the ugly, and the in-between. For example, if you noticed during week #1 you struggled with showing appreciation to GOD, note it. If by week #2 things became easier, note that. There's no shame in having *your* feelings. Remember, they are *your* feelings and GOD already knows how you feel before you're aware of your feelings.

Beloved, during this 30-day exercise don't focus on past hurts. This is not the time for that. Don't mull over anything negative that happened before you started your 30-day journey. Rehashing blessings of the past is ok but stay within the parameters set for this exercise.

Below are a few options you may choose to follow during your 30 days. Divide your 30 days into 3 parts: the past, present, and future.

Option 1 - (10 days) = Thankful for *past* blessings.

Option 2 - (10 days) = Thankful for *present* blessings.

Option 3 - (10 days) = Thankful for *future* blessings.

Another option is to mix and match. Meaning, if you choose option 1, you can include options 2 and 3. So instead of having 10 days for the past, 10 for the present, and 10 for the future, you can include your present and future desires in Part 1(present blessings). For no particular reason at all, I chose the latter. However, you may find it more suitable to list all past blessings for the 1st 10 days before moving on to list present and future blessings. It's all completely optional. Do whatever works best for you. It's all preferential. This is merely a guideline for those who need a structured way to approach their 30-day journey. Another option for those who are searching for the best approach is to designate the current day to either all past, all present, or all future blessings. Meaning, on one day, you'll focus all your thank yous on past blessings, then the next day you may opt to focus your thank yous on your present days' blessings. On the next day, you may give thanks for the present day or you may go back to listing past events. You may choose to list future events. On any day, the objective is, just get it done! As you see, there are various options. Complete mixing and matching is fine.

THE WISER YOU ARE, THE MORE SELECTIVE YOU BECOME IN WHAT YOU SEE.

If you're still wondering how to do this for the next 30-days, it's simple. Every time you want to complain about something, use that very complaint and put '*GOD, thank You for* or *Thank You GOD I am*...' in front of your complaint. For example, you have a 10 a.m. appointment and you're not seen until 1 p.m.! The doctor had an emergency, or the receptionist forgot to tell you the doctor would be late. You're completely frustrated because you took the day off work for your annual visit and now you've spent 3 hours in the waiting room. Yikes! Yeah, I know this is a hard pill to swallow, but remember, there's always something you can be grateful for. Here goes:

GOD thank You for the job I have that I was able to take time off to come to this visit today.

Thank You GOD I can sit and wait for a visit.

Thank You GOD I was able to take myself to the doctor.

Thank You GOD for giving me the patience to wait.

Thank You GOD for giving me compassion to understand that life happens.

GOD thank You for giving me the ingenuity to use this waiting period to catch up on my leisure reading.

Psalm 46:10 says, *"Be still and know that I am GOD: I will be exalted among the heathen, I will be exalted in the earth."* Beloved, be still! In times of distress, anger, disappointment, and unforeseen changes, know that GOD is GOD! He will have His perfect way. He leaves no stone unturned. So even when you feel GOD isn't there or He isn't vindicating for you, don't fear, just trust. The more you complain is the more you'll remain in your situation. To change your situation, enter GOD's court with praise and witness your spirit lift. Don't fear. F.E.A.R. is Fictional Episodes Appearing Right. So exalt and avoid being halted. Praise your way to promotions. Praise your way to joy. Praise GOD and be raised out of the dung heap! Witness your spirit rise. Watch your expectations of yourself raise. Praise your way to changing your life!

"Make a joyful noise unto the LORD all ye lands." The bible clearly tells us in Psalm 100:1, to *make a joyful noise* – a sound unto the LORD. The bible does not say to remain silent, nor does the bible instruct us to grumble or complain unto the LORD.

The bible tells us to "speak those things that are not as if they are. *"(As it is written, I have made thee a father of many nations,) before him whom he believed, even God, who quickeneth the dead, and calleth those things which be not as though they were."* ~ Roman 4:17. You can set yourself up to be slungshot into your dreams by simply verbally expressing gratitude and offering thanksgiving. Don't be shy, testify!

Again, we read in Proverbs 18:21, *"Death and life are in the power of the tongue: and they that love it shall eat the fruit thereof."* The scriptures speak of the power of our words, of being vocal. The bible even speaks of our very thoughts! So even being quiet has an effect. A famous saying and major concept found in the book of Proverbs 23:7 says, *"For as he thinketh in his heart, so is he."* Another scripture and frequently taught principle can be found in the book of Philippians 4:8 where we read, *"Finally, brethren, whatsoever things are true, whatsoever things are honest, whatsoever things are just, whatsoever things are pure, whatsoever things are lovely, whatsoever things are of good report; if there be any virtue, and if there be any praise, think on these things."* If you plan to use your words to change your life, remaining quiet won't benefit you. Be grateful in everything and you will witness doors being opened for you.

During your 30-day journey, make it your business to speak and think only positive words and thoughts. Turn a blind eye to what you feel is bad/negative and speak the opposite. It matters not if others think you're nuts, all that matters is you remain focused on the mission, *30 Days of Gratitude.* You'll be astonished at how you develop a habit of being grateful.

Researchers have said it takes 21 days to form a habit. Well, guess what, you're on a 30- day journey of being grateful, not complaining, or asking GOD for a thing. You're on a 30-day habit-forming journey and this is definitely, without a shadow of a doubt, a habit you want formed.

I intentionally included blank pages so you can draw, write, scribble, cry, pause, or do whatever brings you healing. Just don't stop! Keep going. Let your expressions flow freely, uninhibited, and unrestrained.

Success is the cumulative affect of tiny repetitive actions you commit to daily. I think this is so very appropriate, as it applies to everyday life. It's one of those things I think most people know and have said in *their* sort of way but sometimes seem to forget to apply. During your 30-day journey, hold on to that statement. Let it be a constant reminder that Rome was not built in a day. Let it be a source of encouragement, but always allow GOD to be *your* ultimate source of encouragement.

Gratitude

"There's a harsh awakening,

prior to a mighty awakening."

Day 1 ~ Put To The Test

~ 07.29.2020

GOD, today's July 29, 2020. Time for my manicure & pedicure.

My phone alarmed at 10 a.m. reminding me of my 10:30 a.m. salon appointment. So off I went, rushing to get there on time with the back seat of my car piled high with my packages needing to be returned. I figured I'd go get my mani-pedi before running errands. So, I get to the salon all flustered because I was rushing, only to be told my appointment isn't until 1 p.m.!!! Are you kidding me?! You've got to be kidding me, I said to the salon owner. The owner showed me her appointment book with my name scribbled next to 12:30 p.m. for a pedicure and 1 p.m. for a manicure! I was *so* not happy. I told her I'll get the pedi while I consider waiting for the mani. Honestly, I probably would've left and gone elsewhere if they did my pedi and then needed the chair for someone. Oddly enough, the lovely lady who did the pedicure told me to remain in the seat for a bit. I found that odd because they're usually very busy. Not to mention, that *never* happened before. Granted, this was only my 2nd time visiting this salon. Thankfully, I had the book, *Dream It. Pin It. Live It.* with me. I've been trying to read this book for the past 7 months! Yes, I ordered it at the beginning of the year because it was being offered for free plus shipping and handling. So, I figured, why not get it? I had decided to do a vision board this year and it was the beginning of the year. Yup, a vision board. I did 2 in times past but never really focused on them and before you know it, they always ended up out of sight! One under my bed, and the other in my closet. Also, I never followed any sort of instructions on how to construct a vision board, so this book was ideal. Ok, I know, I'm going off on a tangent. Back on course. Anyhow, I'm glad I brought a book! Yes, I had my phone and I usually watch some sort of Christian motivational video or a sermon, but I decided to read the book! Reading for me tends to be more challenging because of time, unlike listening or even watching something educational.

I sat in the chair after my pedicure from 11 a.m. until 12:30 p.m.! I must say, it was appreciated. I was able to read more of the book. You wouldn't believe where I left off some time ago in the book; I left off at chapter 7, The Law of Attraction In Action: What Are You Currently Attracting? Yes, yes, yes, I know. On the very day I decided to be obedient to GOD and start my 30-days of gratitude journey, it happened to be the same day I began rereading the book. It also happened that I picked up in the chapter discussing gratitude! Now, for those who don't believe in GOD, let me tell you something, the proof is in the pudding! As I often say, there are no coincidences, there are only GOD-incidents! Amen. Now would you say I just *happened* to stop reading after chapter 6? The chapter before the one that focuses on the very assignment GOD gave me, to solely pray with gratitude. Do you think it's coincidental I just *happened* to reconnect with this book on the day I started my 30-day journey? Or maybe you think I just *happened* to pick up at the very chapter dedicated to having an attitude of gratitude?! No, no, no. Nope, not a coincidence, but a GOD-incident. Yup, GOD *is* real! Now since that's settled, let's get back on track.

I hung out a bit more until 1 p.m. and finally it was my turn. My nail technician was so nice and really did an excellent job. He took 1.5 hours to do my *active length* nails. Go figure! Can we just say, attention to details is not a deficit for him? I intentionally keep my nails short because I feel it's professional, plus I can type faster. Wait, don't go thinking I'm complaining because I'm not! I'm so past that! I had a huge knot in my throat while it was all happening. Not to mention, I asked for my nails to be kept at the length they currently were, but hey, I suppose my technician felt I needed them to be *extremely* active length! By the time he was finished, my nails looked like nubs! But nope, no sir, no ma'am, no complaints here although I seriously had that knot in my throat, that felt like it was getting tighter.

I looked at the time and realized, I only have 1 hour before I'm supposed to go sleep. Go figure. I didn't get any of my errands done, but nope, I'm still not complaining. Trust me, those were all the thoughts running through my head, but I seized each one of them. I know self-praise is no praise, but let me just say, I did a pretty great job at reversing my thinking. Of course, I didn't do it on my own! It was all by GOD's great and mighty grace and His strength. As the bible says in Philippians 4:13, I can do all things through Christ who strengthens me! Amen.

Check it out below, my attitude of gratitude. I had an opposite thought for some things I listed for Day 1. The thought that normally would've been a complaint, I turned it into a praise! Happy reading!

1. Thank You GOD I have hands and fingers so I can get a manicure.
2. Thank You GOD I have feet and toes so I can get a pedicure.
3. Thank You GOD I have money to pay for this spa day, $87 later.
4. Thank You GOD for helping me exercise patience.
5. Thank You GOD for helping me realize You're why I can do all the things I've done.
6. Thank You GOD I have a car to drive to this appointment.
7. Thank You GOD for the free *bags* of bread a friend gave me.
8. Thank You GOD for the abundance of bread I was able to share with 2 others.
9. Thank You GOD for my parents and their health.
10. Thank You GOD I have nails that could be cut short.
11. Thank You GOD for the book I am reading.
12. Thank You GOD for confirmation from the book I'm reading that You want me to write *this* book, *30 Days of Gratitude: Use your words to change your life.*
13. Thank You GOD for loving me.
14. Thank You GOD for blessing me.
15. Thank You GOD for always standing by my side.

Your day 1

Title: Time: Date:
_____

Your Day/Feelings/Thoughts/Prayer

"Exalt the Lord our God And worship at His holy hill, For holy is the Lord our God."

– Psalm 99:9

Your day 1

How were you a blessing today? (A kind word or gesture you offered someone.)

What are you thankful for?

1. Thank You GOD
2. Thank You GOD
3. Thank You GOD
4. Thank You GOD
5. Thank You GOD

Your day 1

"Exalt the Lord our God And worship at His holy hill, For holy is the Lord our God." – Psalm 99:9

Day 2 ~ Morning Gratitude

~ 07.30.2020

Jesus, my days sort of run together since I started working overnight.

I feel like I'm always up! Anyhow, I am just grateful for everything GOD is, has, and will do for me. Glory to GOD. I am actually at my desk at work typing this. I may add more later in the day, but at 7:23 a.m. here are the things I am thankful to GOD for. You know, before I even start typing I just want to say, I will never have enough written, spoken, or words to express *all* the things I am grateful to GOD for.

1. Thank You GOD for being excellent!
2. Thank You GOD for just being You!
3. Thank You GOD because You love me despite my flaws.
4. Thank You GOD for who You are.
5. Thank You GOD for another day at work.
6. Thank You GOD for the jobs I have.
7. Thank You GOD that during a time as such, the pandemic, where people have lost their jobs, You see fit to bless me with multiple jobs! My cup runneth over.
8. Thank You GOD I'm at peace with not asking You for anything.
9. Thank You GOD I have joy unspeakable and I'm not 100% sure why.
10. Thank You GOD for speaking so clearly to me.
11. Thank You GOD for having patience with me.
12. Thank You GOD for extending grace unto me.
13. Thank You GOD for never leaving me.
14. Thank You GOD for loving me.
15. Thank You GOD for the great people around me.
16. Thank You GOD for laughter.

17. Thank You GOD for causing others to buy me things even when I tell them not to.
18. Thank You GOD my soul is at peace.
19. Thank You GOD I don't feel worried.
20. Thank You GOD for the great price _You_ secured for the renovation of my bathroom.
21. Thank You GOD for gently correcting me when I typed _I_ instead of _You_ in #20.
22. Thank You GOD for helping me pay closer attention to details.
23. Thank You GOD for life.
24. Thank You GOD I had the finances to get the bathroom done.
25. Thank You GOD for allowing people to trust and confide in me.
26. Thank You GOD that because my ways are pleasing to You, You've made even my enemies at peace with me.
27. Thank You GOD for giving me a smile that's been said to shatter the darkness.
28. Thank You GOD for reminding me no matter how ugly a person is toward me, I am reminded they are made in the likeness of You.
29. Thank You GOD for allowing me to write to Your children.
30. Thank You GOD for speaking to me.
31. Thank You GOD for giving me the words to write.
32. Thank You GOD You help me to not fear transparency.
33. Thank You GOD!

Your day 2

Title: Time: Date:

Your Day/Feelings/Thoughts/Prayer

"For great is the Lord and greatly to be praised; He is to be feared above all gods."

– Psalm 96:4

Your day 2

How were you a blessing today? (A kind word or gesture you offered someone.)

What are you thankful for?

1. Thank You GOD
2. Thank You GOD
3. Thank You GOD
4. Thank You GOD
5. Thank You GOD

Your day 2

"For great is the Lord and greatly to be praised; He is to be feared above all gods." – Psalm 96:4

Day 3 ~ Just Thankful

~ 07.31.2020

Holy Spirit, I slept 8 whole hours and I'm still yawning and tired!

This is pretty much unheard of when it comes to me, sleeping 8 hours, I don't think so! This only happens if I'm sick or haven't slept in 2 or so days. I was seriously tired after my doctor's appointment and hanging in this New York heat! Ok, so it was only about 89 degrees, but for me, that's just too hot! Nevertheless, I had a great day. I went to work, got off, went to my appointment, and then bed. Pretty good if I must say so myself. I have to remember to return my sunglasses, but other than that all is well. Oh wait, tonight I resisted getting something to eat. My last meal was around noonish and then when I woke up for work, of course I was hungry. This week is the 1st week I decided not to eat at night. Not even a piece of fruit! I kinda felt like I was in hibernation. I had to resist. This COVID-19 pandemic hasn't been gracious to my hips! Of course, it wasn't by my willpower, but with the power of GOD! Thank You GOD. Wait, let me save my gratitude for the list!

1. Thank You GOD for loving me.
2. Thank You GOD for blessing me.
3. Thank You GOD for always standing by my side.
4. Thank You GOD for helping me resist eating late at night.
5. Thank You GOD for giving me traveling mercies.
6. Thank You GOD for my health and strength.
7. Thank You GOD for the water I showered with.
8. Thank You GOD for the coffee I'm ready to drink.
9. Thank You GOD for giving me time to write.
10. Thank You GOD for blessing me with relaxing jobs.

11. Thank You GOD for the great people around.

12. Thank You GOD for the free food.

13. Thank You GOD for my car.

14. Thank You GOD for the larger new home.

15. Thank You GOD for my absolutely amazing spouse.

16. Thank You GOD for my blessed, beautiful, and healthy babies.

17. Thank You GOD for my joy.

18. Thank You GOD for my washer and dryer.

19. Thank You GOD for great parents.

20. Thank You GOD for safety.

21. Thank You GOD for insight.

22. Thank You GOD for my health.

23. Thank You GOD for wisdom.

24. Thank You GOD for Your guidance.

25. Thank You GOD I'm actually journaling all of this!!!

Your day 3

Title: _____   Time: Date:
_____

Your Day / Feelings / Thoughts / Prayer

"What? know ye not that your body is the temple of the Holy Ghost which is in you, which ye have of God, and ye are not your own?" – 1 Corinthians 6:19

Your day 3

How were you a blessing today? (A kind word or gesture you offered someone.)

What are you thankful for?

1. Thank You GOD
2. Thank You GOD
3. Thank You GOD
4. Thank You GOD
5. Thank You GOD

Your day 3

"What? know ye not that your body is the temple of the Holy Ghost which is in you, which ye have of God, and ye are not your own?" – 1 Corinthians 6:19

Day 4 ~ I Am Thankful

~ 08.01.2020

Another ordinary day.

Today I worked, went home, ate, and went to bed. Well, maybe not quite like that. I actually completed a work project with a deadline set next week. I'm *so* happy that's behind me.

It's almost 5 a.m. on August 1st and my birthday is just 4 days away. I usually don't make a big to-do about my birthday, but I did start a little tradition of going somewhere new for a few days by myself for *my* special day. This year I wanted to visit Greece. *Yes*, Greece. I know it would be *way* more than my usual few (2-3) days, but that's what I wanted. Who can resist such a picturesque place with beautiful blue waters and pristine white buildings? Not me! Such a scenery definitely attracts me. Loved ones always say, "Why don't you go to Jamaica? You haven't been home in a while." Yes, it's true, I haven't been home in a while, but I decided many years ago I would stop *revisiting* places. I mean, no matter how much I love a place, I'm just not going to keep going there. Sure, Jamaica *is* beautiful. Yes, *I am* Jamaican, and I don't know every nook and cranny in Jamaica, but I would still like to visit some of GOD's *other* beautiful creation. GOD made everything and everyone. I just feel like, why should we limit ourselves to just knowing or learning about the familiar? I mean seriously, how much will you learn about someone or something you are already very familiar with? So no, I don't hate my country. To the contrary, I love my country! As a matter of fact, Jamaican pride is written *all* over me. Can't you see it? Just kidding, but not really. Nevertheless, as a child of GOD, living in New York has helped me crave broadening my horizon. I love GOD, I love His people, and I love learning about various cultures. Now there's the sociologist in me talking!

Enough of my going on about me and what I like, what I think, and blah, blah. It's time to show gratitude. Oh, by the way, I was giving GOD all the praise, glory, and honor on my drive into work. Nothing unusual there. That's my common routine.

1. Thank You GOD for making me, me.
2. Thank You GOD for the coffee I just drank.
3. Thank You GOD for decreasing my appetite.
4. Thank You GOD for increasing my willpower so I don't eat late at night.
5. Thank You GOD for providing a restroom.
6. Thank You GOD for properly functioning bowels.
7. Thank You GOD for giving me peace and serenity.
8. Thank You GOD for a tranquil mind.
9. Thank You GOD for allowing me to be an encourager to my friend who's completing her book.
10. Thank You GOD for my friend Tazetta's life.
11. Thank You GOD for the wonderful people you've sent to encourage me.
12. Thank You GOD for the finances to make home renovations.
13. Thank You GOD for helping me find items to fit perfectly in my home.
14. Thank You GOD for my sanity of mind.
15. Thank You GOD I am increasingly and rapidly losing weight.
16. Thank You GOD I attain my ideal weight.
17. Thank You GOD for my sight.
18. Thank You GOD I can purchase those things I need and want.
19. Thank You GOD I can be a blessing to others.
20. Thank You GOD for not giving me over to a reprobate mind.
21. Thank You GOD for removing the scales from my eyes.
22. Thank You GOD for keeping Your hand on my life.
23. Thank You GOD for Your protection.

24. Thank You GOD for Your continued mercy and grace.

25. Thank You GOD for the hedge of protection You've placed around me.

26. Thank You GOD for answering my prayers.

27. Thank You GOD for teaching me how to pray.

28. Thank You GOD for pulling me closer to You.

29. Thank You GOD for helping me maintain a relationship with You.

30. Thank You GOD for allowing me to know the truth and that truth has a name, Jesus Christ of Nazareth.

31. Thank You GOD for my hearing.

32. Thank You GOD for helping me to walk in forgiveness.

33. Thank You GOD for placing a true prophet in my life.

34. Thank You GOD for the upcoming opportunities.

35. Thank You GOD for allowing me to complete those things that were left undone.

36. Thank You GOD for Your favor.

37. Thank You GOD for reminding me daily of things I ought to be thankful for.

38. Thank You GOD that I am not easily offended.

39. Thank You GOD things of the past don't hurt as they once did.

40. Thank You GOD for an increase in understanding.

41. Thank You GOD for wisdom.

42. Thank You GOD the curse has been broken.

43. Thank You GOD for keeping me in Your secret hiding place.

44. Thank You GOD for my amazing spouse & his family.

45. Thank You GOD for my family.

46. Thank You GOD for each day You remind me of more things to be thankful for.

47. Thank You GOD You've made time for me to complete this book.

48. Thank You GOD for my willingness to be transparent and vulnerable so others can be healed.

Title: Time: Date:

Your Day/Feelings/Thoughts/Prayer

"This is the day the LORD has made, we will rejoice and be glad in it." – Psalm 100:1

Your day 4

How were you a blessing today? (A kind word or gesture you offered someone.)

What are you thankful for?

1. Thank You GOD
2. Thank You GOD
3. Thank You GOD
4. Thank You GOD
5. Thank You GOD

Your day 4

"This is the day the LORD has made, we will rejoice and be glad in it." – Psalm 100:1

Day 5 ~ GOD's Grace

~ 08.02.2020

No matter the obstacles you encounter or the fiery darts the enemy throws, rest assured GOD is and will always remain in control!

GOD is in total control of everything in your life. It becomes apparent more so once you sit back and allow Him to take control. This means, you should always seek His face and identify the benefit in all situations.

Today has been particularly rough. Two blow ups at work that were completely unnecessary. I see this as an opportunity for me to truly exercise my gratitude toward the Most-High. Despite the circumstance, I am, and will forever be grateful to GOD.

1. Thank You GOD for loving me.
2. Thank You GOD for blessing me.
3. Thank You GOD for always standing by my side.
4. Thank You GOD for the ability to remain in control.
5. Thank You GOD for always reminding me of who *You* are.
6. Thank You GOD for helping me not become easily offended.
7. Thank You GOD for showing me who people are.
8. Thank You GOD for the test I endure.
9. Thank You GOD for always watching over me.
10. Thank You GOD for helping me to remain calm.
11. Thank You GOD for helping me to grow.
12. Thank You GOD that nothing bothers me.
13. Thank You GOD for fighting my battles for me.
14. Thank You GOD for who You are.
15. Thank You GOD for giving me *Your* perfect peace.
16. Thank You GOD!

Your day 5

Title: Time: Date:

Your Day / Feelings / Thoughts / Prayer

"And if it seem evil unto you to serve the LORD, choose you this day whom ye will serve; whether the gods which your fathers served that were on the other side of the flood, or the gods of the Amorites, in whose land ye dwell: but as for me and my house, we will serve the LORD."

– Joshua 24:15

Your day 5

How were you a blessing today? (A kind word or gesture you offered someone.)

What are you thankful for?

1. Thank You GOD
2. Thank You GOD
3. Thank You GOD
4. Thank You GOD
5. Thank You GOD

Your day 5

"And if it seem evil unto you to serve the LORD, choose you this day whom ye will serve; whether the gods which your fathers served that were on the other side of the flood, or the gods of the Amorites, in whose land ye dwell: but as for me and my house, we will serve the LORD." – Joshua 24:15

Day 6 ~ Rest

~ 08.03.2020

Talk about a well needed day off!

I had a pretty full day at work on Saturday. I ended up working a double to help out and by Sunday I was completely pooped. With all the construction happening in my house, I feel displaced. So, I managed to rest a little, but then had to run around and buy some tiles to complete the bathroom. Other than that, it was a pretty peaceful day.

1. Thank You GOD for rest.
2. Thank You GOD for providing the finances needed to renovate.
3. Thank You GOD for the vehicles we have.
4. Thank You GOD for great friendships.
5. Thank You GOD for simply being You.
6. Thank You GOD for watching over me as I sleep.
7. Thank You GOD for protecting my home.
8. Thank You GOD for protecting my parents.
9. Thank You GOD for all the blessings You have bestowed on me.
10. Thank You GOD for always listening to me.

Title: _____   Time: Date:
_____

Your Day/ Feelings/ Thoughts/ Prayer

"Saying, Amen, blessing and glory and wisdom and thanksgiving and honor and power and might, be to our God forever and ever. Amen." – Revelation 7:12

Your day 6

How were you a blessing today? (A kind word or gesture you offered someone.)

What are you thankful for?

1. Thank You GOD
2. Thank You GOD
3. Thank You GOD
4. Thank You GOD
5. Thank You GOD

Your day 6

"Saying, Amen, blessing and glory and wisdom and thanksgiving and honor and power and might, be to our God forever and ever. Amen." – Revelation 7:12

Day 7 ~ GOD Never Fails

~ 08.04.2020

Here it is, my birthday week and it seems the hounds of hell have been unleashed!

Hey, guess what, I bind every spirit not of Holy Spirit in the mighty and matchless name of Jesus Christ of Nazareth! Amen! So that settles that!

I hope you're still reading. It's really that easy. Think about it, every situation whether good or bad appears first in the spiritual realm (world) before you encounter it in the physical realm. Therefore, everything that happens in the physical, must be dealt with in the spiritual. Meaning, *use your words to change your life*! *Listen*, using words, especially GOD's Word, is one of the most powerful weapons in your arsenal. This is true on all levels. Think of a time when you argued with someone you love, and they said something very hurtful. Think back to how their words pierced your core. It wasn't a physical touch that affected you, but instead, it was their words that shook you to the core. Think of how long it took you to get over what was said.

Some words scar some people so deeply, they have to seek counseling to move beyond the hurt. Again, it wasn't a blow of the fist that caused the pain, instead, it was the utterance of a person's word(s) that wounded deeply.

Use your words wisely. Treat your words as if they are gold! Most people wouldn't just throw gold around or be careless with it. Most would try to secure their gold and even keep it polished. They would give it extra care. So why not give your words extra care? Why not treat your words as if they are gold? Begin saying, "*My words are golden!*" Remember, the power contained in words don't discriminate. It is the same power harnessed regardless how the words are used. Whether your aiming to inflict pain and incite destruction or cause healing, joy, laughter, and spread love, your words have power! The effect is contagious. Words can affect yourself and others. When you speak life over yourself, life is what *you'll* receive. When you speak life over another, life is what *you'll both* receive. This principle is known as the law of sowing and reaping. Galatians 6:7 says, "…for whatsoever a man soweth, that shall he also reap."

Think of a time when someone doubted your ability to do something and told you you can't do it. Their doubting your ability to succeed, caused you to believe you can't succeed. Their spoken words made you think you're incapable, and as such, you did nothing. Now, think of another time when someone else or maybe even that same person said you couldn't do something, but *you* said, "Watch me do it," and bingo, you got it done! Beloved, you spoke it into the atmosphere and it manifested, period! You spoke it, and it happened! Now use that same energy, that same belief, that same iron clad determination, and ruthless perseverance to change your life! Use *your* positive words as a rudder and steer your life in the direction you wish it to go.

An old Jamaican adage I've heard all my life is, "A closed mouth doesn't get fed." Pretty much self-explanatory, right. If you don't open your mouth, you won't get what you need or want.

Today, GOD gave me the idea for this book's cover. I normally don't think about the cover until the end, but I spoke to the artist 2 days ago and asked him to think of something clean for this cover. I'd never done that before. I've always said what I'd like, and he'd move things around according to my leading. However, this time, I think I've just been really tired, and I didn't feel like thinking. Ha! Go figure. Anyhow, after speaking with him 2 days ago, I decided I needed to continue doing as I normally do, seek the LORD and trust that He will give me the cover design. Well, there you have it, the LORD *gave* me the design for the book cover today! It's simple, it's clean, and I know once it's done, I'm gonna absolutely love it! I mean, when GOD gives you something, of course it's grand! Thank You Abba.

1. Thank You GOD for giving me wisdom.
2. Thank You GOD for giving me insight.
3. Thank You GOD for giving me the words to speak.
4. Thank You GOD for teaching me how to use my words appropriately.
5. Thank You GOD for always being by my side.
6. Thank You GOD for giving me the idea for this book cover.
7. Thank You GOD for being You!
8. Thank You GOD for always coming through for me.
9. Thank You GOD when I feel alone, You remind me how much You love me.
10. Thank You GOD for fighting *all* my battles.
11. Thank You GOD weeping endures for a night, but joy comes in the morning.
12. Thank You GOD that what the enemy meant for evil, You turned it for my good.
13. Thank You GOD for making things simple for me.
14. Thank You GOD for my growth.
15. Thank You GOD for spiritually maturing me.
16. Thank You GOD I am not offended.
17. Thank You GOD for those who love me.
18. Thank You GOD for giving me advice when I am not asking.
19. Thank You GOD for answering even when I don't know to ask.
20. Thank You GOD for Your continued mercies.
21. Thank You GOD for loving me.
22. Thank You GOD for blessing me.
23. Thank You GOD for always being by my side.
24. Thank You GOD.

Your day 7

Title: Time: Date:

Your Day/Feelings/Thoughts/Prayer

"O Lord, You are my God; I will exalt You, I will give thanks to Your name; For You have worked wonders, Plans formed long ago, with perfect faithfulness." – Isaiah 25:1

Your day 7

How were you a blessing today? (A kind word or gesture you offered someone.)

What are you thankful for?

1. Thank You GOD
2. Thank You GOD
3. Thank You GOD
4. Thank You GOD
5. Thank You GOD

Your day 7

"O Lord, You are my God; I will exalt You, I will give thanks to Your name; For You have worked wonders, Plans formed long ago, with perfect faithfulness." – Isaiah 25:1

Day 8 ~ The Number Of New Beginnings

~ 08.05.2020

On this day, a beautiful real-life baby doll – as my mom said strangers would say to her while she was holding me – was born to Errol and Winnie Mattis! Yes. I am fearfully and wonderfully made and so are you!

What a blessing it is to be alive and still have all my faculties. I have been so blessed! My word. Today is my birthday and the number of wonderful birthday wishes I've gotten, definitely reminds me of how loved I am. What a blessing. My friend, who doesn't celebrate birthdays, came from North Carolina with her hubby to spend the day with me. I so appreciate her. She did my hair, we laughed, drove around, and enjoyed each other's company. It was great!

My parents, of course, gave me the most beautiful heartfelt cards ever! Of course cash was included. My dad's traditional to the core and old school machismo, but he wrote some of the most beautiful words. It was lovely. While mom of course always comes through with such lovely cards. I am blessed! Obviously, by now you realize I am a words person, so cards mean a lot to me.

Friends from all over called and it was beautiful. I am blessed!

Yesterday I went for my yearly mammography, and I received a call to return for additional scanning. They said my right breast is dense and they need to do an ultrasound and another mammo. Dense?! Hum. Hey, believe it or not, I am not worried. The day before my birthday they say this and the day after my birthday I'll go for the 2nd appointment. Worried? Not at all. I know I am blessed! GOD's got this!

1. Thank You GOD for loving me.
2. Thank You GOD for blessing me.
3. Thank You GOD for always standing by my side.

4. Thank You GOD for a great bill of health.

5. Thank You GOD for an excellent sono and mammo report tomorrow.

6. Thank You GOD for finances to enjoy each day.

7. Thank You GOD for making me absolutely beautiful inside and out.

8. Thank You GOD for making me who I am.

9. Thank You GOD for my home.

10. Thank You GOD for my parents and their health.

11. Thank You GOD for helping me have joy.

12. Thank You GOD for not allowing me to have a heavy heart.

13. Thank You GOD for teaching me how to express gratitude.

14. Thank You GOD for teaching me how to love.

15. Thank You GOD for this wonderful man who is my future husband.

16. Thank You GOD.

Title: Time: Date:

Your Day/Feelings/Thoughts/Prayer

"You are my God, and I give thanks to You; You are my God, I extol You."

– Psalm 118:28

Your day 8

How were you a blessing today? (A kind word or gesture you offered someone.)

What are you thankful for?

1. Thank You GOD
2. Thank You GOD
3. Thank You GOD
4. Thank You GOD
5. Thank You GOD

Your day 8

"You are my God, and I give thanks to You; You are my God, I extol You." – Psalm 118:28

Day 9 ~ GOD First. Sophia Second

~ 08.06.2020

When you're faced with a difficult situation and can easily react according to your flesh. you must remember who you are and whose you are.

I *am* a child of GOD no matter the circumstance. I must always choose GOD over the flesh.

So I came into work jovial, rested, and happy to be at work. I was moving along throughout the office saying my routine hi's when I encountered one coworker who became pretty abrupt and out of order pretty fast. He proceeded to ask me why I had the right to do something that no one else was allowed to do. Now before you go on to say that's because of GOD's favor, in this instance what his mind told him was happening, really wasn't happening at all. I was not the only person doing something everyone else was not allowed to do. I was doing what some of the others should have been doing. Nevertheless, I entertained his series of questions, responding as peaceably as possible until I felt I hit a wall. He continued to ask the same questions repeatedly. Knowing the conversation wasn't going anywhere, I decided to disengage. One question I asked him was if during my 2 days off they made him a supervisor. Of course, he said no. He looked very embarrassed and quite uncomfortable during his reply. I then proceed to inform the lead on his team of his behavior and continued my day. Normally I would've been pleased and patted myself on the back because I refrained from going haywire, but this time I wasn't. I wasn't pleased with the fact that I questioned him in such a manner, knowing it would've caused him to become embarrassed. Yes, Jesus was very direct, oftentimes speaking in parables, and was notorious for upsetting the applecart, but his intentions were never ill. Truth be told, my intentions were ill. Yes, that doesn't sound nice, I know, but full disclosure is what this journey is all about. He offended me and so I decided to clap back. No one is perfect, even if they try to have others think so. When you sit back and say something to someone you know will cause them to be embarrassed – translation, hurt – that is never a good thing. So even right now, I must take a moment to say, "LORD GOD, I repent of my sin. Please forgive me for not being an upstanding person in Your sight. Please help me to never miss the mark You've placed for me. Help me turn from my wicked ways and always exemplify Your Son, my LORD, and Savior, Jesus Christ of Nazareth. In Jesus Christ of Nazareth's name, I pray, Amen.

Ok so wait, I just *asked* GOD for something. I just *asked* for forgiveness, I *asked* Him to help me never miss the mark. I *ask*ed Him to help me turn from my wicked ways. Beloved, I just asked, asked, and asked again when GOD told me not to ask for anything. Listen, truth be told, I could've and really wanted to stop typing and delete the first ask, but I decided to leave it. I decided to continue being the honest person I always strive to be. Since this is a 30-day journal of my daily encounters, in which I chose to be transparent, I decided to continue. Hum, I wonder if it's ok to ask for forgiveness and GOD's help in making me a better person? Sounds rather silly, doesn't it? Well, no matter how silly it sounds, it's really food for thought. Think about it, if GOD said for 30 days don't ask me for anything, just be thankful, then I believe that doesn't exclude all I just asked for. A little tricky isn't it and if you were here with me right now as I type, you would see my eyebrows scrunched up as I'm in deep thought.

Alright, let's see, I asked for forgiveness, and I repented. So, I asked for forgiveness and all the other things. I think I may have missed the mark today with the *not asking* for anything, even as subtle as it sounds. Now I'll turn it around and thank GOD for everything, as I was instructed to do. Hey, even right now could be an opportunity for me to ask GOD for forgiveness of not following His instructions, but nope, I'm definitely not going to fall into that trap again. I mean look at how easy it is for us to miss the mark. So here goes.

1. GOD thank You for being so gracious to me.

2. GOD thank You for being so understanding.

3. GOD thank You for always standing by my side.

4. Thank You GOD for Your protection.

5. Thank You GOD for Your wisdom.

6. Thank You GOD for insight, wisdom, and discernment.

7. Thank You GOD for my quiet time.

8. Thank You GOD for allowing me to realize my flaws.

9. Thank You GOD for pointing out my frailty.

10. Thank You GOD for reminding me of who You are.

11. Thank You GOD for reminding me I am made from dust!

12. Thank You GOD for humbling me in spirit.

13. Thank You GOD my heart has not grown cold.

14. Thank You GOD that despite how I am treated, I often default to, what would Jesus do?

15. Thank You GOD for my job.

16. Thank You GOD for greater later.

17. Thank You GOD for reminding and helping me not despise small beginnings.

18. Thank You GOD for keeping my mind on, "Are my ways pleasing to You?"

19. Thank You GOD for a repentant heart because all have fallen short of Your glory.

20. Thank You GOD You've taught me not to live in condemnation, but instead, to accept conviction.

21. Thank You GOD for teaching me the difference between condemnation and conviction.

22. Thank You GOD for giving me understanding of many things.

23. Thank You GOD for loving me even when I'm being unlovable.

24. Thank You GOD for success.

25. Thank You GOD for making me a trustworthy person.

26. Thank You GOD for golden opportunities.

27. Thank You GOD for helping me see the glass as half full instead of half empty.

28. Thank You GOD for safety.

29. Thank You GOD.

Your day 9

Title: Time: Date:

Your Day/Feelings/Thoughts/Prayer

"I will praise the name of God with song And magnify Him with thanksgiving." – Psalm 69:30

Your day 9

How were you a blessing today? (A kind word or gesture you offered someone.)

What are you thankful for?

1. Thank You GOD
2. Thank You GOD
3. Thank You GOD
4. Thank You GOD
5. Thank You GOD

Your day 9

"*I will praise the name of God with song And magnify Him with thanksgiving.*" – Psalm 69:30

Day 10 ~ Somber Spirit

~ 08.07.2020

Today I feel a bit somber in spirit.

I don't mean to go backward, but I feel compelled to include this. When GOD tells you not to ask for anything and you're following suit, GOD *still* allows room for help! What a mighty GOD we serve. Through it all, GOD definitely has a sense of humor.

Isn't it wonderful to have a friend who will cheat for you? Listen, hear me out before you start getting bent outta shape. So, I told my friend about the day I had yesterday, (which was really the same day, I just didn't journal this) and she said well let's pray. Her prayer consisted of asking for things from GOD on my behalf. That's what we Christians call intercession or 'standing in the gap' for someone. She asked for protection and to destroy all evil sent to me from wherever it came from. Basically, without going into everything she prayed for on my behalf, just know she prayed asking the Father for things for me. That's what I mean by cheating! So, although I'm not supposed to ask GOD for anything for the next 30 days, now 20 days, my friend asked for me! I love it! And no, I don't think we're getting over on GOD. Not even for a millisecond! We can't outsmart or outdo the Father nor would I ever try. GOD already knew all of this would take place before it did.

1. Thank You GOD for loving me.
2. Thank You GOD for blessing me.
3. Thank You GOD for always standing by my side.
4. Thank You GOD for an elevated mood.
5. Thank You GOD for bringing me to work safely.
6. Thank You GOD for watching over me.
7. Thank You GOD for watching over my parents.

8. Thank You GOD for always being by my side.

9. Thank You GOD for great relationships.

10. Thank You GOD for peace at work.

11. Thank You GOD for providing me with the finances necessary to fix my car.

12. Thank You GOD for sending me to the right mechanic who's not a rip off.

13. Thank You GOD for this coffee that's helping me stay awake.

14. Thank You GOD for a broken cycle of poverty.

15. Thank You GOD for simply being You!

16. Thank You GOD.

Your day 10

Title: Time: Date:

Your Day/Feelings/Thoughts/Prayer

"Because Your lovingkindness is better than life, My lips will praise You." – Psalm 63:3

Your day 10

How were you a blessing today? (A kind word or gesture you offered someone.)

What are you thankful for?

1. Thank You GOD
2. Thank You GOD
3. Thank You GOD
4. Thank You GOD
5. Thank You GOD

Your day 10

"Because Your lovingkindness is better than life, My lips will praise You." – Psalm 63:3

Day 11 ~ Be Reminded

~ 08.08.2020

I know what I'm about to say doesn't apply to my experience for the day, but it applies overall.

As it pertains to getting ahead, it's often said, "It's not what you know, but who you know." It's funny, but as I sat here and closed out this very document, preparing to open *Epistles to Abba: Letters From the Heart,* I heard the soothing voice of the LORD say, "It's not what you know, but who you know." So, I sat still in the quiet of the morning continuing to listen. With each breath I breathed and with every stroke of the clock, I wondered, where is the Father going with this. Suddenly, after about a minute or 2, the Holy Spirit calmly brought to my remembrance what someone said to me not too long ago. Someone said, "You will not be promoted because a certain person doesn't know you." Although this was said a few times, it never fully registered until about the 3rd time. At that point, I heard the Holy Spirit say, "And yet you were promoted."

Romans 8:28 ~ [28] *"And we know that all things work together for good to them that love God, to them who are the called according to his purpose."* Beloved, I say this as a reminder to everyone reading this book who feels they're not where they could've been because they didn't know the right person or they weren't born with a silver spoon in their mouth, *you do know the right person*! Well, that's if you know the true and living GOD YESHUA HaMashiach – Salvation and The Anointed One. The Father reminded me if a person knows Him, GOD, He's *the only one* they need to know. If GOD be for you, who can be against you?! For GOD *is* the ultimate source. Romans 8:30-31 [30] *"Moreover whom he did predestinate, them he also called: and whom he called, them he also justified: and whom he justified, them he also glorified. [31] What shall we then say to these things? If God be for us, who can be against us?"*

1. Thank You GOD for loving me.
2. Thank You GOD for blessing me.
3. Thank You GOD for always standing by my side.
4. Thank You GOD for making me perfect.
5. Thank You GOD for always guiding me.
6. Thank You GOD!

Title: Time: Date:

Your Day / Feelings / Thoughts / Prayer

"to the only wise God, through Jesus Christ, be the glory forever. Amen."

– Romans 16:27

Your day 11

How were you a blessing today? (A kind word or gesture you offered someone.)

What are you thankful for?

1. Thank You GOD
2. Thank You GOD
3. Thank You GOD
4. Thank You GOD
5. Thank You GOD

Your day 11

"to the only wise God, through Jesus Christ, be the glory forever. Amen." – Romans 16:27

Day 12 ~ A And My. A Subtlety

~ 08.09.2020

It's the little things that can sometimes be major.

Every blessing from the LORD is a major blessing. I recall hitting a huge pothole and could swear I felt it in my stomach. I continued driving to work, not thinking anything of it. Low and behold, about a few weeks to a month later, at 35mph, my car started vibrating! I admit, I am a bit of a fast driver, but 35mph is extremely slow for me. The vibration kept me at that speed because I was worried about the shaking and the sound coming from my car was concerning. Yup, muffler issues! When it rains, it pours. So, finally, I decided to take my car to the mechanic. He said it's a balancing issue. I was pretty excited to know I wouldn't pay an exuberant amount of money. I spent $100 bucks and that included a pack of tints, car freshener, and the price for balancing. I was stoked! Then the mechanic told me my flex pipe needed changing and it wouldn't cost that much. I took the car to one guy who was too busy to even stop and look at me so I walked out. I went to another shop where the owner told me the flex pipe and another portion of the muffler needed to be cut out and replaced. He said it will take less than 1 hour and cost $200 flat! So for $300, my car was fixed and off I go, carrying on with my routine! Thank You sweet LORD! Oh, and might I add, it turns out that my mechanic's wife is co-owner of a bookstore in Jamaica! Ding, ding, ding, ding, ding. I struck gold! I've been trying to get my book into a bookstore in Jamaica and just like that, voila, co-owner of a bookstore appeared! Well, I should say, the connection appeared. So now, I'll have a few of my books, *Christianity 101: The ABC's and 123's of The Faith, plus Epistles to Abba: Letters From The Heart, and* this very book, *30 Days of Gratitude: Use Your Words to Change Your Life* in the store! Come on now, you can't tell me GOD ain't grand!

I remembered saying to the mechanic, no, I don't have children yet. I'm doing right by GOD, which means I am waiting for a husband first. Then I asked him to pray for a husband for me. Well what came next was surprising. He said no! I was shocked! He said I will *not* pray for a husband for you. I asked him why and he said, "I won't pray for *a* husband for you because I will not ask GOD to have you commit adultery." I was baffled! He then explained, for me to pray for a husband for you that would mean he is already married, and you will be committing adultery. Ooohhh, I said, having that lightbulb moment. Then I said, you're right, please pray for a good man for me and he said, aahhh, now you've got it!

Wow, all these years I've been asking for a husband, and I think this was the time the LORD decided to use him to show me that I am asking incorrectly. What I meant and what I was saying, were two different things.

To GOD be all the glory, for He and He alone is more than worthy of *all* our praise! Amen.

Jesus! As I sit here trying to conclude, I just heard the Holy Spirit say, "This is why all the men who come your way are always married." OH MY GOODNESS! What an epiphany! Now it all makes sense! I wondered why so many married men were attracted to me. It began to bother me, and I thought maybe this is some sort of test, but clearly it wasn't! Clearly it was me, getting exactly what I asked for! Thank You Holy Spirit for direct revelation and no thank you *universe* for sending me this request although it's what I asked for!

1. Thank You GOD for loving me.
2. Thank You GOD for blessing me.
3. Thank You GOD for always standing by my side.
4. Thank You GOD for all these blessings.
5. Thank You GOD for making the issue with my car a simple fix.
6. Thank You GOD for teaching me how to pray without asking for things.

7. Thank You GOD for always giving me favor.

8. Thank You GOD for peace.

9. Thank You GOD for tranquility.

10. Thank You GOD for the good people around me.

11. Thank You GOD for the amazing man destined to be *my* husband.

12. Thank You GOD for placing people in my life to remind me to be careful how I speak.

13. Thank You GOD for highlighting the subtle spoken negativities.

14. Thank You GOD for my rapid and healthy weight loss.

15. Just thank You GOD for being You! Amen.

Title: Time: Date:

Your Day / Feelings / Thoughts / Prayer

"Suddenly a great company of the heavenly host appeared with the angel, praising God and saying, "Glory to God in the highest heaven, and on earth peace to those on whom his favor rests." – Luke 2:13-14

Your day 12

How were you a blessing today? (A kind word or gesture you offered someone.)

What are you thankful for?

1. Thank You GOD
2. Thank You GOD
3. Thank You GOD
4. Thank You GOD
5. Thank You GOD

Your day 12

"Suddenly a great company of the heavenly host appeared with the angel, praising God and saying, "Glory to God in the highest heaven, and on earth peace to those on whom his favor rests." – Luke 2:13-14

Day 13 ~ A Bulletproof Strategy

~ 08.10.2020

A good day.

Today was pretty good. Although stressful at times, work was good. This project I have to do regarding COVID-19 regulations per state seems to be a bit time-consuming. So I did some research, it took me 4 hours and I was feeling pretty good about my accomplishment until I sent a progress report to my director. Lo and behold my director said he had a different template with multiple variables I didn't have! I was floored! When I saw the email with the updated variables, I thought, wow, and just when I was feeling good thinking, I was making headway. Now this is a whole new can of worms. A new project starts tomorrow once I'm home. Sigh. Nevertheless, I thank GOD for job opportunities, especially during a time when many are unemployed.

Nothing much to report here today other than when I put my clothes on, everything felt really snug! Oh my goodness I have to do something a.s.a.p. COVID pounds is no joke and I must reverse this! The overnight shift definitely sabotages a girl's figure. But GOD! The LORD will help me get all of this under control. Despite stopping the eating at night thing and waiting for breakfast, the hounds are having a fiasco! O.k., that's enough! I'll be seriously investing in my health starting next week! Why not this week you may be wondering? Well, that's because the concept of what to do entered my mind on Saturday. Today is Sunday and I'm thinking on some things. I want to say what I've been thinking, but I think I'm going to wait. Let's see how things pan out by month-end and maybe then I'll say what it is. Don't worry, it's nothing crazy, it's something necessary. I will say this, I bought a gel seat for my mountain bike. Did I mention how much I love cycling? Just one issue, the seat is not kind to my bum! I pray this new seat will be bum friendly. I just must decide when to start and incorporate it into my day. Oh, I almost forgot, I need a helmet. I'll snag one from the neighborhood sporting goods store. This famous sporting goods store is closing! They've been in my neighborhood since I was a babe. Since COVID, many stores just can't hold on. Truth be told, they were sort of struggling before the pandemic, so I'm not surprised they are closing. Nevertheless, I'll miss them. I'm sad about the store closing. Some of my childhood memories will be wiped away.

1. Thank You GOD for loving me.
2. Thank You GOD for blessing me.
3. Thank You GOD for always standing by my side.
4. Thank You GOD for my weight loss.
5. Thank You GOD for my health strategy.
6. Thank You GOD for insight.
7. Thank You GOD for the finances to do what I have to do.
8. Thank You GOD for encouragement.
9. Thank You GOD for new beginnings.
10. Thank You GOD for filling my heart with You.
11. Thank You GOD for rest.
12. Thank You GOD for peace.
13. Thank You GOD for laser-sharp focus.
14. Thank You GOD for balancing my life.
15. Thank You GOD I belong to You.
16. Thank You GOD for new opportunities.
17. Thank You GOD for the success of this book.
18. Thank You GOD for the success of all books You've birthed out of me.
19. Thank You GOD for being on time.
20. Thank You GOD for simply being You!

Title: Time: Date:

Your Day/Feelings/Thoughts/Prayer

"O magnify the Lord with me, And let us exalt His name together." – Psalm 34:3

Your day 13

How were you a blessing today? (A kind word or gesture you offered someone.)

What are you thankful for?

1. Thank You GOD
2. Thank You GOD
3. Thank You GOD
4. Thank You GOD
5. Thank You GOD

Your day 13

"O magnify the Lord with me, And let us exalt His name together." – Psalm 34:3

Day 14 ~ Be Still And Know I Am GOD

~ 08.11.2020

Regardless of how things appear, be still, and know that GOD is GOD.

It was a bit of a rough day. It was my first day back and things seemed different. A little tension and not the usual happy space I'm used to. It's amazing how you can forget about the happenings of the day if you just offer up a prayer, laugh some, and rest.

I called a friend who is grounded in the Word and told her of the issues that happened. She spoke life into my spirit and continued to minister positivity into the situation. Simply put, when an army comes against you, be still, and know that GOD *is* GOD. Psalm 46:10 ~ *"Be still and know that I am God: I will be exalted among the heathen, I will be exalted in the earth."*

1. Thank You GOD for just being You!
2. Thank You GOD for sending me help.
3. Thank You GOD for great parents.
4. Thank You GOD for the love You've surrounded me with.
5. Thank You GOD for my car.
6. Thank You GOD for safety.
7. Thank You GOD for watching over me.
8. Thank You GOD for your prophets.
9. Thank You GOD for always being You.
10. Thank You GOD for resurrected friendships.
11. Thank You GOD for never leaving me in the storm.
12. Thank You GOD for loving me.
13. Thank You GOD for blessing me.
14. Thank You GOD for always standing by my side.
15. Thank You GOD.

Your day 14

Title: Time: Date:

Your Day/Feelings/Thoughts/Prayer

"They raise their voices, they shout for joy; They cry out from the west concerning the majesty of the Lord." – Isaiah 24:14

Your day 14

How were you a blessing today? (A kind word or gesture you offered someone.)

What are you thankful for?

1. Thank You GOD
2. Thank You GOD
3. Thank You GOD
4. Thank You GOD
5. Thank You GOD

Your day 14

"They raise their voices, they shout for joy; They cry out from the west concerning the majesty of the Lord." – Isaiah 24:14

Day 15 ~ GOD To The Rescue

~ 08.12.2020

When GOD comes to the rescue you know you're saved!

I talked to a wonderful man of GOD, who's truly anointed to speak the word. He said things that encouraged and blessed my socks off. It's always nice to have someone speak positive things to you especially after being a bit downtrodden. I thank GOD I have the freedom to write this. Blessed be the name of GOD. He is more than worthy of *all* our praise!

Zephaniah 3:17 ~ *"The LORD thy God in the midst of thee is mighty; he will save, he will rejoice over thee with joy; he will rest in his love, he will joy over thee with singing."*

The second part of my day was consumed with deliverance. Some of you may be wondering, what is deliverance? Deliverance is what a Christian call being set free from those things which are not of GOD. Things like smoking, alcoholism, depression, witchcraft, and all things not of GOD. You can do self-deliverance if you have the know-how or you can receive deliverance via one who is saved and knows how to do deliverance. To be clear, it is GOD who delivers us by way of the person doing the deliverance. In my case, I have undergone both. I've done self-deliverance and have had both deliverance and non-deliverance ministers intercede on my behalf. Now you may be wondering, well if she was delivered before, why did she go through deliverance again? Easy, that's because deliverance is a lifetime feat. We're living in a world where things can corrupt us. As such, we need to seek GOD's help in setting us free from the many evils we encounter. We need GOD's help to set us free from the things we allow to grab hold of us. One deliverance minister equated deliverance to peeling an onion. She said, just as an onion has many layers, that's the same way we have many layers needing to be peeled. What she meant was you can be set free from one thing or even a series of things, but there remain more things needing to be uprooted and abolished. As such, a need is never fully resolved while we're in the flesh.

1. Thank You GOD for loving me.
2. Thank You GOD for blessing me.
3. Thank You GOD for always standing by my side.
4. Thank You GOD for the victory.
5. Thank You GOD for surprising me.
6. Thank You GOD for reinventing me.
7. Thank You GOD for encouraging me.
8. Thank You GOD for blessing me.
9. Thank You GOD for being patient with me.
10. Thank You GOD for making a way of escape for me.
11. Thank You GOD for never giving up on me.
12. Thank You GOD for always investing in me.
13. Thank You GOD for clarity of mind.
14. Thank You GOD for peace and serenity.
15. Thank You GOD for always protecting me.
16. Thank You GOD for giving me ingenuity.
17. Thank You GOD for giving me the weight-loss remedy.
18. Thank You GOD for my success.
19. Thank You GOD for my wealth.
20. Thank You GOD for my creativity.
21. Thank You GOD!

Title: Time: Date:

Your Day/Feelings/Thoughts/Prayer

"Worthy are You, our Lord and our God, to receive glory and honor and power; for You created all things, and because of Your will they existed, and were created."

– Revelation 4:11

Your day 15

How were you a blessing today? (A kind word or gesture you offered someone.)

What are you thankful for?

1. Thank You GOD
2. Thank You GOD
3. Thank You GOD
4. Thank You GOD
5. Thank You GOD

Your day 15

"Worthy are You, our Lord and our God, to receive glory and honor and power; for You created all things, and because of Your will they existed, and were created." – Revelation 4:11

Day 16 ~ From Dark To Light

~ 08.13.2020

Whatever is in the dark will surely come to light.

<u>Luke 12:2-5</u> ~ *²"For there is nothing covered, that shall not be revealed; neither hid, that shall not be known. ³ Therefore whatsoever ye have spoken in darkness shall be heard in the light; and that which ye have spoken in the ear in closets shall be proclaimed upon the housetops. ⁴ And I say unto you my friends, Be not afraid of them that kill the body, and after that have no more that they can do. ⁵ But I will forewarn you whom ye shall fear: Fear him, which after he hath killed hath power to cast into hell; yea, I say unto you, Fear him."*

I'm always in awe of the power and magnificence of the Almighty. When someone plans your demise, it is so wonderful to sit back and watch the Father work on your behalf. Sometimes you're completely unaware of the storm brewing, but thank GOD He's never unaware. He remains on the throne and will *never* be dethroned! GOD doesn't wear pajamas!

To protect certain individuals and not cause chaos, I will tell this scenario in a round-about way. When you're doing your best to live an upstanding life and others who profess the name of Jesus come and try to sabotage you, it can be quite devastating, to say the least. It's important to understand there are sheep in wolves' clothing who have been strategically placed in certain places to be a pitfall for the non-vigilant or baby Christian.

Jealousy, envy, greed, and ego all play a very wicked role in the grand scheme of things with the one who is attempting to bring you down. Jealousy is not of GOD neither are any of the other things I just listed above. Jealousy is what caused Saul to chase David around to kill him. Jealousy is what caused Saul to fall! Jealousy is what caused Josephs' suffering which propelled him to the top! Jealousy and wickedness caused Judas Iscariot to sell out Jesus of Nazareth for a mere 30 shackles! Jealousy, although vile and ungodly, helped pushed many to the top! I said all of that to say, when someone is planning to harm you, GOD has already planned to secure you. When you love the LORD and you're walking with GOD, sure, you may suffer a little scuff here and there or maybe a mighty scuff, but ultimately, GOD will not allow your demise.

It's funny how the very plan the enemy concocted for me, GOD stepped in as maestro. Everything was perfectly orchestrated. Every piece of the puzzle was put together to work in my favor. Yes, I was fuming when I learned of the situation and how the person totally manipulated numerous people to get to me! I should've been calm, but truth be told, I was ticked off! No, I didn't sin in my anger, but I sure felt like I could've easily blown a gasket! Nevertheless, after I spoke a little and made a few moves, all of what happened ended up working out in my favor.

To GOD be all the glory! I also learned of a lie that was told which caused major chaos. This pushed all the heat toward me! I was shocked and upset, to say the least. Nevertheless, again I say, what the enemy meant for evil, GOD turned it around for my good! Thank You Abba for loving me. Indeed, I am the apple of GOD's eye.

1. Thank You GOD for loving me.
2. Thank You GOD for blessing me.
3. Thank You GOD for always standing by my side.
4. Thank You GOD for revelation.
5. Thank You GOD for exposing the enemy.
6. Thank You GOD for restoration.
7. Thank You GOD for lightening my workload.
8. Thank You GOD for rest.

9. Thank You GOD for helping me not sin when angry.

10. Thank You GOD for always blessing me.

11. Thank You GOD I am the apple of Your eyes.

12. Thank You GOD for wisdom.

13. Thank You GOD for clarity.

14. Thank You GOD for divinely orchestrating my life.

15. Thank You GOD for simply being You!

Your day 16

Title: Time: Date:

Your Day/ Feelings/ Thoughts/ Prayer

"and he said with a loud voice, "Fear God, and give Him glory, because the hour of His judgment has come; worship Him who made the heaven and the earth and sea and springs of waters." – Revelation 14:7

Your day 16

How were you a blessing today? (A kind word or gesture you offered someone.)

What are you thankful for?

1. Thank You GOD
2. Thank You GOD
3. Thank You GOD
4. Thank You GOD
5. Thank You GOD

Your day 16

"and he said with a loud voice, "Fear God, and give Him glory, because the hour of His judgment has come; worship Him who made the heaven and the earth and sea and springs of waters." – Revelation 14:7

Day 17 ~ Peace After The Storm

~ 08.14.2020

For I know the thoughts I think of you says the LORD.

Jeremiah 29-11~ *"For I know the thoughts that I think toward you, saith the LORD, thoughts of peace, and not of evil, to give you an expected end."*

Sometimes you kick and scream when things don't go the way you expected, but beloved, I tell you this, learn to be easy, relax, and know that GOD is GOD *all* by Himself. GOD doesn't need yours, mine, or anyone's help to make choices. His ways and thoughts are higher than our ways and thoughts period, full stop! We can trust GOD, knowing all decisions made on our behalf when we pray are all based on GOD's will. Let His will be done and not your will be done. Ultimately beloved, if your will is done, more than likely, things will need to be undone!

I can recall desperately wanting a certain situation to happen and with all I tried, nothing came of it. I wondered, why GOD, why? Yet there was no answer. Truth be told, I don't even think I went to GOD to ask why. However, I do know I said, "GOD if it is Your will, let it be done." I was ashamed, angry, bitter, and not acting Godly, to say the least. I had misplaced anger. I became angry with 3 people who were granted the very thing I was believing I would've received. Anyhow, after a few days of not being Christ-like, the Father dealt with me. He dealt with my emotions! I heard that still soft voice say, "It's not their fault." Yup, you guessed it, *the voice*, although still, calm, and loving, hit me like a ton of bricks! Isn't it funny how GOD can just utter a few words and those very words seize you on the spot! Beloved, believe it or not, as soon as I heard the voice of the Holy Spirit, my mind began to change. I think within a few hours, my progressively hardening heart, began softening. Yes brethren, just like that, once again my heart became supple! As time went by, I found myself not caring. I returned to the jovial Sophia I used to be. I became the Sophia people knew me to be.

Fast-forward to months later, I was in the presence of many of the people who witnessed what happened, and yet I felt nothing! They all decided to say how I looked good, and one even said I look like I lost weight! I mean, seriously?! I actually gained weight. Nevertheless, the mere fact they all thought I looked good was just more proof of GOD's greatness. He said He would give me beauty for ashes! He said no good thing would He withhold from me. When I felt I was in the dung heap and shriveling away, the LORD picked me up and helped me breathe again with these 4 words, "It's not their fault." With those simple words, the Father helped me dust myself off, regain my identity, and move on. How great is our GOD!

So, my beloved, remember this, when life is happening, as I like to say, remind yourself, "It's not their fault." Even if you think it *is* their fault, as difficult as this may sound, remind yourself it's the spirit in the person, it's not actually the person.

1. Thank You GOD for loving me.
2. Thank You GOD for blessing me.
3. Thank You GOD for always standing by my side.
4. Thank You GOD for extending grace unto me.
5. Thank You GOD for being patient with me.
6. Thank You GOD for a speedy recovery.
7. Thank You GOD for not allowing my heart to remain hard.
8. Thank You GOD for always embracing me.
9. Thank You GOD for Your continued mercies.
10. Thank You GOD I don't look like what I've been through.
11. Thank You GOD for Your grace.
12. Thank You GOD for sheltering me.
13. Thank You GOD for watching over me.
14. Thank You GOD for speaking to me.
15. Thank You GOD for being so great!

Title: Time: Date:

Your Day/Feelings/Thoughts/Prayer

"Who will not fear, O Lord, and glorify Your name? For You alone are holy; For all the nations will come and worship before You, For Your righteous acts have been revealed." – Revelation 15:4

Your day 17

How were you a blessing today? (A kind word or gesture you offered someone.)

What are you thankful for?

1. Thank You GOD
2. Thank You GOD
3. Thank You GOD
4. Thank You GOD
5. Thank You GOD

Your day 17

"Who will not fear, O Lord, and glorify Your name? For You alone are holy; For all the nations will come and worship before You, For Your righteous acts have been revealed." – Revelation 15:4

Day 18 ~ Because GOD Is Not Stagnant

~ 08.15.2020

Why does GOD have me doing 30 days of gratitude?

While speaking with one of my confidantes, I asked that very question. Not to say I'm questioning the Father, but just wondering what wonderful work the LORD is doing in me. I mentioned to a friend that maybe GOD is saying this is a form of deliverance and I need to be delivered. That thought came about after my friend said, "Writing down your day and what you've gone through is a form of deliverance." She said many people can't do this because they have trouble letting go of things. I completely agreed as we both spoke about how we used to struggle with forgiveness. Thank GOD He has delivered us from that. Then I went on to say to her that it could very well be why the Father has me doing 30 days of gratitude. I also said it could be the LORD spiritually taking me to a higher level because normally the fleshly man prays requesting things from GOD, but He instructed me to pray with an attitude of gratitude. Just thanking Him for what He has and *is* doing is the highest form of praise.

Brethren, I tell you this, we never know what we're capable of doing until the Father places a mandate on us. What do I mean? Most people pray asking GOD for things unless they hear the Father say, "For 30 days, don't ask Me for anything," as in my case. Then suddenly, you realize you can actually pray and fellowship with the Father by solely thanking GOD. You begin to thank Him for the things He has done, is doing, or you desire for Him to do. I've learned that instead of asking GOD for something, no matter the dire need, just turn the ask into a thank you. That is exactly what I explained in the intro of the book. Then I thought, wait a minute, I have friends asking me to pray and sometimes GOD is telling me to pray for them, yet I am not to ask for anything. So what did I do? I followed the unction of Holy Spirit and thanked GOD for everything they require.

One friend's mom isn't doing well, and she asked me to pray for her mom's healing. I prayed, thanking GOD for her healing. Let me pause and point out, when praying as such, the LORD can use this as a faith-building exercise. Yes, beloved, it is a faith-building exercise. How so, you may be wondering? Think of it like this, when you pray thanking GOD for the very thing you desire yet don't already have, that is you believing GOD to bring into physical existence the thing which is present in the spiritual. Hebrews 11-1 says, *"Now faith is the substance of things hoped for, the evidence of things not seen."*

See how the Father is helping me and all who choose to pray in such a manner. It's a faith building exercise. It's quite ingenious for sure and only GOD Himself could've thought of something like this. Praying as such is also a way to bring you to another level in your walk with GOD. Doing so helps you mature in the faith, strengthen your relationship with GOD, and rely on the Father for *all* things.

Now, as you chronicle your day just as I'm doing, this will help you see how GOD is working in your life. I believe, as we're busy going about our day, sometimes we fail to recognize the blessings the Father bestows upon us, rarely taking time to reflect on the happenings of the day. However, when we write things down, it helps still the mind long enough to reflect on the goodness of the LORD.

I can imagine the thoughts some of you are having. You may be saying, "But I had an awful day! What's the blessing in this day?!" My answer is, you're still alive and breathing! That *is* a blessing!

Think of Joseph whose brothers left him for dead. Although he was jailed, he ended up becoming 2nd in charge of Egypt. Think of Moses, his mom put him in a basket, sent him up the river thinking she'd never see her baby again, only to later be summoned to nurse him who later had her son help set their people free. Think of Esther, she was orphaned, raised by her uncle Mordecai, and later was chosen by king Ahasuerus of Persia to be his queen. Esther was strategically placed by GOD for a later time to help save the Jewish people. Then the most profound of all, think of King Jesus of Nazareth who was born to later be crucified/sacrificed so all who believe in Him and profess Him as LORD and Savior over their life will have eternal life with the Father! I can go on, but I believe you get the picture. All those people during their traumatic day, at some point, probably felt it was one of, if not, the absolute worst day of their life! The bottom line is, GOD works all things together for the good of those who love Him and are called according to His purpose. Amen. *"And we know that all things work together for good to them that love God, to them who are the called according to his purpose."* ~ <u>Romans 8:28</u>. So, the next time *you feel* your day is terrible, pause, and reflect on those examples. Blessings and love beloved.

1. Thank You GOD for loving me.
2. Thank You GOD for blessing me.
3. Thank You GOD for always standing by my side.
4. Thank You GOD for being the epitome of truth.
5. Thank You GOD for being all-wise and sharing Your wisdom with me.
6. Thank You GOD for daily revelation.
7. Thank You GOD for deliverance.
8. Thank You GOD for making things so clear to me.
9. Thank You GOD for helping me to put things into proper perspective.
10. Thank You GOD for You *are* Mighty!

Title: Time: Date:

Your Day/Feelings/Thoughts/Prayer

"And every created thing which is in heaven and on the earth and under the earth and
on the sea, and all things in them, I heard saying, "To Him who sits on the throne, and
to the Lamb, be blessing and honor and glory and dominion forever and ever."

– Revelation 5:13

Your day 18

How were you a blessing today? (A kind word or gesture you offered someone.)

What are you thankful for?

1. Thank You GOD
2. Thank You GOD
3. Thank You GOD
4. Thank You GOD
5. Thank You GOD

Your day 18

"And every created thing which is in heaven and on the earth and under the earth and on the sea, and all things in them, I heard saying, "To Him who sits on the throne, and to the Lamb, be blessing and honor and glory and dominion forever and ever." – Revelation 5:13

Day 19 ~ The Fruits Of Your Labor

~ 08.16.2020

It pays to be kind.

    This isn't the days' event, but I feel lead to discuss it. My moment of transparency. I fell behind with my journaling for 5 days! Yes love, I was completely inundated with work, my car having minor issues, and so I became completely fatigued trying to juggle it all. I thank GOD for His grace. It's not an excuse to let things slip but thank GOD for grace. Not to mention, I had quite a few eventful days at work. Whew, thank GOD for a new day, a new week, a new me, a new grace! Yes, every day, GOD gives us new grace to deal with the day. <u>Lamentations 3:22-26</u> reads, *"It is of the LORD's mercies that we are not consumed, because his compassions fail not. [23] They are new every morning: great is thy faithfulness. [24] The LORD is my portion, saith my soul; therefore will I hope in him. [25] The LORD is good unto them that wait for him, to the soul that seeketh him. [26] It is good that a man should both hope and quietly wait for the salvation of the LORD."*

    I recall a coworker being let go. For what reason, I don't know. I was pretty distraught about it because this particular person seemed to have a stellar way about them. They were kind, reserved, friendly, helpful, and understanding. Just a wonderful person to work with. Anyhow, the person was let go and it took me about 2 weeks to simmer down. I probed trying to find out why they were let go, but just got fluff on all sides. Anyhow, immediately upon finding out about their termination, I phoned them and offered to pray for them. The person was upset, gave me their side of what they felt caused the termination, and couldn't understand what happened. I called to be a shoulder of support and provide consolation. They showed total gratitude for what they called an act of kindness. I felt Holy Spirit tell me to pray for the person and so I did.

That very prayer solidified in their mind who they surmised me to be. They said they thought I was a good person but now they know for fact, I am. As time went on and I continued to check on the person, I received a call from this individual asking me to join them in a particular endeavor. I was floored! Completely honored, I surely wasn't expecting anything in return! The individual said to me, "You see what being kind to someone can do for people." They thanked me for my kindness, expressing heartfelt gratitude for the prayer I said, and stated they felt the prayer in their core. I was so excited to know the prayer I offered to the Father on their behalf, helped to ease the weight they felt from being terminated.

I was so very excited, surprised, and honored to be offered an opportunity to partake in an endeavor with this individual. What a blessing it is to be obedient unto the LORD. What a blessing it is to see the fruits of your labor! Amen.

1. Thank You GOD for You are great!
2. Thank You GOD for Your magnificence.
3. Thank You GOD for showing me how to pray.
4. Thank You GOD for allowing me the opportunity to be a blessing.
5. Thank You GOD for blessing me.
6. Thank You GOD for loving me.
7. Thank You GOD for always standing by my side.
8. Thank You GOD for Your faithfulness.
9. Thank You GOD for giving me a heart of compassion.
10. Thank You GOD for making me care.
11. Thank You GOD for Your graciousness.
12. Thank You GOD for always being there.

Title: Time: Date:

Your Day/Feelings/Thoughts/Prayer

"I will give thanks to You, O Lord my God, with all my heart, And will glorify Your

name forever." – Psalm 86:12

Your day 19

How were you a blessing today? (A kind word or gesture you offered someone.)

What are you thankful for?

1. Thank You GOD
2. Thank You GOD
3. Thank You GOD
4. Thank You GOD
5. Thank You GOD

Your day 19

"I will give thanks to You, O Lord my God, with all my heart, And will glorify Your name forever." – Psalm 86:12

Day 20 ~ As Harmless As A Dove

~ 08.17.2020

Our behavior should always reflect the gospel of Christ and supported with words if your behavior isn't evident of the gospel.

Preach the gospel at all times. Our behavior should always reflect the gospel of Christ and supported with words if your behavior isn't evident of the gospel. I heard something similar to my statement on the radio on my drive into work tonight. I was in a bit of a somber mood and didn't feel like going to work, but knew I had to. I fully started enjoying my 3 days off. I was able to get so much done on those days. Sure, I was pretty wiped out by the end of the week, but it's so well worth it to be able to stay home and tend to the things of GOD, like writing this journal! Hey, let me tell you, I am super excited about this book! Not to say I wasn't about the others, but this one is a workbook! It's my very first workbook. Although my friend suggested I publish a study guide, I never did because I didn't get that nudging from Holy Spirit. It's a great idea, but I suppose the timing wasn't right. However, now GOD said red light, green light, go and so I went. Well not exactly. I didn't hear Holy Spirit say, red light, green light, go. That's just me saying so! I did hear Holy Spirit say, "Don't ask for anything during the next 30 days. Just give GOD praise, journal your day, put it in a book, and make it a workbook! Bam, just like that, in that order! I said all of that to say, I am stoked about getting this book out. I suppose it's also because I am an active learner. I like to write when I read and study, so structuring this book as a workbook has me jumping for joy.

Back to my day. I wrapped up some of my work and headed to bed by 6:30 p.m. only to have to wake up by 10:30 p.m.! I was telling myself I won't have enough rest to carry me through the night, but so far so good. It's 4:46 p.m. and only 4 hours to go. Almost there and I'm still typing. Thank You, GOD! I woke up at exactly 9 pm. I never made it to the 10:30 p.m. mark. I slept less than 3 hours and was fully awake. I looked around wondering why am I awake? I wondered why I didn't feel tired. After lying in bed for about 5 minutes, I jumped up and decided to start reading. What I'm reading I'll keep secret for now because it's a surprise. I'll share that with you in a future book. For now, just know that GOD definitely encouraged me to get the book and start reading. This book for sure is essential to my future writings and all. Talk about on time! Well, the Father saw a need to nudge me, helping me with time management. He helped me realize I will be doing what a very wise friend advised. Once I was finished reading, I got myself together for work and felt pretty wonderful. I should've patted myself on the back. Now I just have to stick to it. With GOD's grace, I will be able to stick to it. With GOD's grace, I will be tremendously successful with this endeavor.

Look at GOD y'all. This is day 20 of my 30 days of gratitude journey and GOD is answering and revealing. He is strategically placing all the pieces of my puzzling life together. Thank You GOD.

I just had an epiphany; well should I say Holy Spirit dropped this into my spirit. I just heard the Holy Spirit say, "You asked for this." What was Holy Spirit referring to? Holy Spirit was reminding me that I was excited to work on the overnight shift when I was having thoughts of how long I will do this overnight thing. It was just a thought and I think it was pretty much a fleeting thought. However, it's not the Father's desire for us to have our minds consumed with anything outside of Him and His will. So I believe one reason the Spirit of the LORD whispered to my spirit, is that as I was typing my 30 days of gratitude segment, my mind wandered a bit to a change in shift. Yes, I believe GOD wants me to remain focused on His task and nothing else and He'll take care of everything that concerns me. Matthew 6:33 ~ *"But seek ye first the kingdom of God, and his righteousness; and all these things shall be added unto you."*

Wait a minute, I mentioned displaying the sort of behavior that reflects the gospel of Jesus Christ for a reason. I brought it up to say this, someone lied on me and caused a shift in the emotions of some people toward me. This lie was revealed during this 30-day journey, and I was pretty upset. I decided at the last minute to address it and then stopped. It's not the first I've heard it, but every time I do, it galvanizes my spirit. It makes me remember who GOD has called me to be. After hearing that, I decided to take a more subtle approach. I confronted the one who lied. Yeah I think it's better to say it that way as opposed to, I confronted the liar! I digress. I confronted the one who lied and expressed exactly how I felt. They extended an apology and I accepted. Now it's time for me to move on. Major damage was done, and time is needed to reverse the trail of devastation left behind, but GOD! All I have to do is, forgive, express love, and be as wise as a serpent, and as harmless as a dove. Matthew 10:16 ~ *"Behold, I send you forth as sheep in the midst of wolves: be ye therefore wise as serpents, and harmless as doves."*

1. Thank You GOD for loving me.
2. Thank You GOD for trusting me to share Your thoughts.
3. Thank You GOD for wisdom.
4. Thank You GOD for your guidance.
5. Thank You GOD for teaching me patience.
6. Thank You GOD for helping me extend grace.
7. Thank You GOD I am not holding a grudge.
8. Thank You GOD no ill feelings linger.
9. Thank You GOD for taking on my yolk.
10. Thank You GOD for placing a smile on my face despite the circumstance.
11. Thank You GOD for working everything out for my good.
12. Thank You GOD for helping me continue to trust You.
13. Thank You GOD for showing me I'm maturing spiritually.
14. Thank You GOD for making me as wise as a serpent and as harmless as a dove!
15. Thank You GOD.

Your day 20

Title: _____ Time: _____ Date: _____

Your Day / Feelings / Thoughts / Prayer

"Keep your behavior excellent among the Gentiles, so that in the thing in which they slander you as evildoers, they may because of your good deeds, as they observe them, glorify God in the day of visitation." – 1 Peter 2:12

Your day 20

How were you a blessing today? (A kind word or gesture you offered someone.)

What are you thankful for?

1. Thank You GOD
2. Thank You GOD
3. Thank You GOD
4. Thank You GOD
5. Thank You GOD

Your day 20

"Keep your behavior excellent among the Gentiles, so that in the thing in which they slander you as evildoers, they may because of your good deeds, as they observe them, glorify God in the day of visitation." – 1 Peter 2:12

Day 21 ~ Supernatural Weapon

~ 08.18.2020

Gratitude is a supernatural weapon.

No matter how you feel, GOD speaks. My first day back to work after an extended weekend of well-needed rest, I enter my space, set up for my shift, and then remembered a beautiful colleague of mine told me she left me a gift. She left the gift on Monday thinking I would be in that night, but I took off. Well, lo and behold, Holy Spirit did it again. He reminded me of the present awaiting me. Oddly enough, I figured it would be some sort of journal, book, or stationary. I love everything involving writing. So bam, a lovely card and book awaited me. My birthday present! It's a belated gift, but I believe it was right on time for me. I opened the card and the written words were beautiful and sincere. You know, sometimes GOD puts 2 people together and both realize they are a match made in heaven. What a blessing from day one and what a blessing I trust they will continue to be. Anyhow, back to this gift and GOD speaking. I usually open books randomly, intentionally just flipping through it. So I opened it as I normally do with all books, flipping through and of course, the very first thing my eyes read was the title of chapter 10. The book opened to the first page of chapter 10 entitled, "Gratitude Is a Supernatural Weapon." Go figure, who would've thought I'd open to this very chapter? I had no idea what the book was about nor had I heard of the author, but GOD surely knew this book would be a right on time book for me. I'm almost finished reading *Dream It. Pin It. Live It.* and was wondering what I would read next. Well GOD answered that question for me. As a matter of fact, the LORD is currently confirming 3 things to me. 1 – Gratitude is what He wants me focused on. Hence, I opened to that chapter. 2 – My photo I like with a serious face. It's the photo a friend said I look angry in, which turned out to be ok to have on my book. The author of this new book has a very serious facial expression. Additionally, she also has a blue shirt on which looks like a jean shirt. This happens to be the same sort of jean shirt I have on in my photo with the serious face! Then 3 – This is the next book I should read. It was gifted right as I am about to complete Terri's book! Now you know this is the next book on my agenda. Look at GOD. I didn't even have to ask the Father what to read next. I have 40 pages left to read in the current book I'm reading and then I'm finished. I've made it my goal to start reading some of the many books I have which are all now collecting dust! One step at a time. Gotta finish my current book first then on to the next! I'm pretty motivated to get it done now. Not to say I wasn't before, but I think I have to push to make it happen. Either way, nothing happens before its time.

So there I go, seriously derailing from the topic. Back on track. I just thank GOD for all He's done. Truth be told, I think I'm rambling a bit because my mind is on journaling what happened when I woke up. Yes, I am journaling sort of backward, but it's ok. I skipped my event for yesterday and moved on to the next day, well sort of. Ok, so none of that matters. What matters is I'm giving it all to you as my day unfolds.

Beloved, know this, just when you feel GOD's not listening or He's not speaking, know that's the furthest thing from the truth. GOD is your best friend in the entire world! Think of how you can't wait to tell your best friend about what happened to you on any given day. Think of how you even tell your best friend how your day was boring or how you were excited or how someone angered you or how you felt totally loved and on top of the world! Think of GOD in the same way but to an unfathomable degree! Honestly, you shouldn't have anyone higher or more important than GOD. He is to be your everything on all levels in all ways. GOD sees and knows all. Remember, He's the one who will *never* turn against you. How gracious is GOD to answer your question(s) before you ask? How gracious is GOD to guide you before you can even think about needing guidance? How gracious is GOD to remind you He is always listening. How gracious is GOD to assure you He cares about everything that concerns you. How gracious is GOD to even think of you! By the way, I think I'll start reading the other book beginning with chapter 10!

1. Thank You GOD for thinking of me even when I am not aware.
2. Thank You GOD for answering the questions I presently can't ask.
3. Thank You GOD for being true to me.
4. Thank You GOD for always letting me know You are listening.
5. Thank You GOD for blessing me.
6. Thank You GOD for taking away all my cares.
7. Thank You GOD for reminding me they hated Jesus first.
8. Thank You GOD for guiding me.
9. Thank You GOD for protecting me.
10. Thank You GOD for always helping me speak truth.
11. Thank You GOD for never leaving nor forsaking me.
12. Thank You GOD for giving me a plan.
13. Thank You GOD for giving me peace.
14. Thank You GOD for giving me rest.
15. Thank You GOD for making me, me!
16. Thank You GOD.

Your day 21

Title: Time: Date:

Your Day/Feelings/Thoughts/Prayer

"So the crowd marveled as they saw the mute speaking, the crippled restored, and the lame walking, and the blind seeing; and they glorified the God of Israel."

– Matthew 15:31

Your day 21

How were you a blessing today? (A kind word or gesture you offered someone.)

What are you thankful for?

1. Thank You GOD
2. Thank You GOD
3. Thank You GOD
4. Thank You GOD
5. Thank You GOD

Your day 21

"So the crowd marveled as they saw the mute speaking, the crippled restored, and the lame walking, and the blind seeing; and they glorified the God of Israel."

– Matthew 15:31

Day 22 ~ Deciding What Not To Do

~ 08.19.2020

Cherish great friends.

Today I went to breakfast with a friend of mine who's such a gift from GOD. He's super funny, wise, kind, patient, and just about all the other good things one would desire in a friend. No, he's not perfect, but he's perfectly made just for me. How I cherish having great people around me. I definitely appreciate having such amazing people around. Thank You GOD for great relationships.

As I continued reading my book today, I got a boost of encouragement once again. I have about 20 pages to go in the book and I'm finished! It's a bittersweet moment because I've thoroughly enjoyed reading the book. I'll forever be grateful. I started developing the good habit of reading something motivational or as some may call it, a self-help book for a few minutes per day. I also started listening to my morning Christian sermon. Those are 2 habits I definitely need to stick to. It's funny how I love reading and have tons of books, but I can barely find time to read. No more! GOD led me straight to the book I needed to read to give me the jumpstart and conviction to start reading again, but this time reading daily.

I came across so many wonderful quotes while reading. I mean they are the sort of quotes that really stick to you. One quote runs in the vein of you knowing what to do and what not to do are equally important. This is so true! Sometimes it's the simple things that are said that hit you the hardest. What a thought, right. You know, it's just a reiteration of what most of us already know. For some, it's probably an ah ha moment for you. It sure was one for me.

1. Thank You GOD for this day.
2. Thank You GOD for allowing me the opportunity to learn something new.

3. Thank You GOD for taking me to work safely.

4. Thank You GOD for great friends.

5. Thank You GOD for always watching over me.

6. Thank You GOD for continually speaking to me.

7. Thank You GOD for clarity and clarification.

8. Thank You GOD for this book, *30 Days of Gratitude: Use Your Words to Change Your Life*. I know it will be a mighty blessing.

9. Thank You GOD for the process of this book which is richly blessing me.

10. Thank You GOD for always standing by my side.

11. Thank You GOD.

Title: *Time:*   *Date:*

Your Day/Feelings/Thoughts/Prayer

"Be anxious for nothing, but in everything by prayer and supplication, with thanksgiving, let your requests be made known to God; [7] and the peace of God, which surpasses all understanding, will guard your hearts and minds through Christ Jesus." – Philippians 4:6-7

Your day 22

How were you a blessing today? (A kind word or gesture you offered someone.)

What are you thankful for?

1. Thank You GOD
2. Thank You GOD
3. Thank You GOD
4. Thank You GOD
5. Thank You GOD

Your day 22

"Be anxious for nothing, but in everything by prayer and supplication, with thanksgiving, let your requests be made known to God; [7] and the peace of God, which surpasses all understanding, will guard your hearts and minds through Christ Jesus." – Philippians 4:6-7

Day 23 ~ To Be Christ-like

~ 08.20.2020

What do you do when GOD says one thing and man says another?

That seems like a simple enough question with a simple answer, right? Well, you'd think so, but it's not so for many. Yesterday, I had 3 encounters dealing with race. It's pretty common and expected during this time. This is the year when a black man by the name of George Floyd was murdered by a police officer while other officers stood around, watched, and did nothing (let me say allegedly to avoid any possible legal ramifications.) Meanwhile, the bystanders were yelling for the officer to stop and screaming, "He can't breathe!" The officer had his knee on Mr. Floyd's neck until Mr. Floyd could no longer breathe. He died in the presence of bystanders. The incident was recorded by the bystander(s). The video went viral (throughout the internet) like a flame in the presence of gasoline. This caused a massive uproar resulting in protests, lootings, killings, and a racial war throughout the world. The purpose of me telling you all of this is not to talk about race wars or the sort, it's merely to set the tone for this days' story and to provide the story for those who will read this after I'm long gone. I feel Holy Spirit telling me to mention this, "Explain what occurred because this book will outlive you. Many may never know the story of Mr. George Floyd." Let me pause to say countless blacks have been murdered and nothing has come of it nor have many people heard of it, but this is the story I'll focus on to build upon yesterday's encounters.

Yesterday started with me discussing GOD with a young lady. We talked about various ministers of the Gospel when she stated, "I don't really like the white preachers." Shortly thereafter, I spoke with an older woman who said, "I don't support white evangelists." She said they are all supporting Donald Trump, the current president of the United States of America. Both ladies speak mainly of things favoring blacks. Then later when I spoke with a male friend, he discussed whites and mentioned various things that I don't necessarily think it's fitting for this book. Anyhow, during each conversation, I felt a little cringe in my spirit. All 3 persons are respectable and quite notable in their respective communities, both foreign, and domestic. All 3 are people I respect. Nevertheless, while all 3 spoke, I wondered, why GOD?! We are to love all people. All were created by You. We should know as Christians it's the spirit in the person which governs their behavior and not the individual. My male friend is not a Christian but watches both white and black Christian televangelists daily. The other 2 friends are Christians. Oddly enough, I said to them, I watch all evangelists who teach sound doctrine. Why was I even having that conversation with Christians? I know tensions are running very high, but as Christians, we are not to get caught up with race wars. We are to stand for GOD and let me be specific, Jesus Christ of Nazareth! I tell everyone, I'm team Jesus! Why didn't I say anything? Why'd I remain silent? I know I'm usually extremely vocal to the point where one of my sisters says I am confrontational. Whenever I call to tell her something happened between myself and someone else, she laughs. When I ask her why she's laughing, she usually says something like, "You're confrontational. There's nothing wrong with it because I'm confrontational as well, but I think you are a little more confrontational than me." So again, why didn't I say anything? One would think I agree with how they feel but to the contrary. I do not! I don't think *all* Caucasians are racist, bad, and hate black people. Nope, not at all. My maternal grandfather is half German and my great grandfather is German! My maternal grandmother is Indian and German and my great grandmother is Indian. Nevertheless, that's a moot point. The bottom line is, I know within every race evil rear its ugly head. That goes for every race! So why didn't I say anything? I don't know. As a matter of fact, I did say something to all 3, but I don't think I spoke strong enough and with full conviction which is completely unacceptable for me. Anyhow, as this is now water under the bridge, I know the opportunity will present itself again for me to speak up. I'm in awe because I'm known for telling people, I'm on no one's side.

I'm on team Jesus. They usually respond by saying, "I hear that!" Despite the laughter, I am as serious as serious can be.

1. Thank You GOD for convicting me.
2. Thank You GOD for making a way out of no way.
3. Thank You GOD for always blessing me.
4. Thank You GOD for presenting me with opportunities to be better.
5. Thank You GOD for always guiding me.
6. Thank You GOD for being that still soft voice that convicts me.
7. Thank You GOD for being gentle with me.
8. Thank You GOD for all You do!
9. Thank You GOD.

Title: Time: Date:

Your Day/ Feelings/ Thoughts/ Prayer

"and for the Gentiles to glorify God for His mercy; as it is written, "Therefore I will give praise to You among the Gentiles, And I will sing to Your name." – Romans 15:9

Your day 23

How were you a blessing today? (A kind word or gesture you offered someone.)

What are you thankful for?

1. Thank You GOD
2. Thank You GOD
3. Thank You GOD
4. Thank You GOD
5. Thank You GOD

Your day 23

"and for the Gentiles to glorify God for His mercy; as it is written, "Therefore I will give praise to You among the Gentiles, And I will sing to Your name." – Romans 15:9

Day 24 ~ GOD's Still In The Miracle Business

~ 08.21.2020

Some people don't believe in miracles. Some people don't believe in GOD. I believe in both!

One of my projects for work was due today. It was extremely tedious, to say the least! I actually spent a good amount of time working on this project and the payout doesn't equate. Anyhow, it's done and I will have a conversation with my director about the length of time such things will take. I may need to scale back. Anyhow, this won't become a gripe session. It's all good. GOD blessed me with an invaluable opportunity linked to this project and what I'll say is, thank You GOD! I mentioned that whole event because my day was consumed by this, both literally and figuratively. All-day I kept thinking of this project because the deadline was today! Thank GOD I met the deadline. I had a challenging time ascertaining the information. I mean, I had to dig and then dig some more! So today as I was sweating wondering how I'm going to get this done, finally, with about 2 hours to spare, I heard Holy Spirit say, "You know someone who lives in those states." Bells, whistles, fireworks, and the like all went off! I couldn't believe it! All along I sat mulling over how to accomplish the task and at the last minute, I heard Holy Spirit speak!!!!! Before I knew it, I was calling and bugging all the people I know who qualified, and before I knew it, I was done! Just like that! Bada boom, bada bang! Can you believe it, so simple yet my mind never thought of it! Look at GOD! Then I started wondering, if GOD wanted to see me sweat! Just kidding. Maybe GOD was just showing me He's still in the business of performing the miraculous? I believe the latter. GOD is always doing miracles. We just need to acknowledge them and be grateful. Amen.

1. Thank You GOD for my miracle.
2. Thank You GOD for making my project so easy.
3. Thank You GOD for reminding me.

4. Thank You GOD I really don't have to ask for anything because You'll just do.

5. Thank You GOD for clarity of mind.

6. Thank You GOD for sustained energy to do all You've called me to.

7. Thank You GOD for the anointing.

8. Thank You GOD for my life.

9. Thank You GOD for always speaking to me!

10. Thank You GOD I am truly blessed.

11. Thank You GOD for helping me be a continued blessing.

12. Thank You GOD for preparing me to be a greater blessing.

13. Thank You GOD for keeping Your hand on my life.

14. Thank You GOD for always standing by my side.

15. Thank You GOD for never leaving or forsaking me.

16. Thank You GOD for my spouse who matches me like a perfectly fitting glove!

17. Thank You GOD for my children who You've blessed and highly favored!

18. Thank You GOD I am blessed!

19. Thank You GOD for 30 Days of Gratitude!

Title: _____   Time: Date:

Your Day/Feelings/Thoughts/Prayer

"Not to us, O Lord, not to us, But to Your name give glory Because of Your lovingkindness, because of Your truth." – Psalm 115:1

Your day 24

How were you a blessing today? (A kind word or gesture you offered someone.)

What are you thankful for?

1. Thank You GOD
2. Thank You GOD
3. Thank You GOD
4. Thank You GOD
5. Thank You GOD

Your day 24

"Not to us, O Lord, not to us, But to Your name give glory Because of Your lovingkindness, because of Your truth." –
Psalm 115:1

Day 25 ~ To And Fro

~ 08.22.2020

It was a long day at work but quite fulfilling.

It's always nice to be appreciated. The staff I work with on the morning shift often expresses their gratitude for me staying behind to help. Since they are so short-staffed, I decided I would help as long as I can. I stay pretty isolated because the company doesn't want us to mix for fear of spreading COVID. It's a wise idea and I agree. This method is called cohorting, where you group the same persons together to decrease the chances of cross-contamination/infection. Anyhow, it's always a pleasure working with them.

One of my other colleagues and I hashed out some of our differences today. It was a relief and pretty peaceful, but truth be told, I don't think my colleague is really over everything although I am. Unfortunately, I can't change the mind of others. Only GOD can do that. My heart is clean and my soul is at rest.

After work, I did the solo breakfast thing. My friends live in different states and my parents are homebodies to the core, especially dad! Nothing wrong with that, but after working all night in a windowless office, coming home from work, sleep, and repeat, I decided to break up the monotony. Yes, I'm a homebody to the core also, but not when I get no outside time. Sun helps make the heart happy. Hey, don't worry, I'm not complaining. During a time of COVID-19 with so many dying, I'm not your eager beaver trying to run to and fro.

1. Thank You GOD I enjoy my own company.
2. Thank You GOD for teaching me how to peaceable agree to disagree.
3. Thank You GOD for Your embrace.
4. Thank You GOD for what You have in store for me.

5. Thank You GOD for sunshine.

6. Thank You GOD for being so great!

7. Thank You GOD for change.

8. Thank You GOD for rest.

9. Thank You GOD, You totally understand me.

10. Thank You GOD for peace and serenity.

11. Thank You GOD I don't stay stuck in my feelings.

12. Thank You GOD for those who love and appreciate me.

13. Thank You GOD for love everlasting.

14. Thank You GOD for the perfect spouse You've ordained for me.

15. Thank You GOD for life eternally.

Your day 25

Title: Time: Date:

Your Day/Feelings/Thoughts/Prayer

"So the crowd marveled as they saw the mute speaking, the crippled restored, and the lame walking, and the blind seeing; and they glorified the God of Israel."

– Matthew 15:31

Your day 25

How were you a blessing today? (A kind word or gesture you offered someone.)

What are you thankful for?

1. Thank You GOD
2. Thank You GOD
3. Thank You GOD
4. Thank You GOD
5. Thank You GOD

Your day 25

"So the crowd marveled as they saw the mute speaking, the crippled restored, and the lame walking, and the blind seeing; and they glorified the God of Israel." – Matthew 15:31

Day 26 ~ Royalty

~ 08.23.2020

Only GOD can make someone treat you like royalty.

I finally caught up with some rest. I didn't feel completely rested, but I definitely wasn't falling on my face! I had a manicure and pedicure appointment and didn't feel like going but knew I needed to. This was one of the days I had some free time. I went to my appointment and my manicurist, who doesn't do pedicures, did my pedicure!! He did a spectacular job! He's known for taking his time and being extremely meticulous, which I fully appreciate. My toenails are shaped perfectly! Then as I was preparing to walk to the manicure table, he took me by the hand and walked me along the aisle as a queen! The looks I got! If looks could kill, I'd be as dead as a doorknob a million times over! Even I was surprised. He walked me to the seat, fluffed the pillow, and off he went to do a marvelous manicure! Ombre with glittered grey. Totally breathtaking in my opinion. I came home, had something to eat, and called it a night. I was pretty pooped. I wanted to work on my book, *Epistles to Abba: Letters From the Heart,* which will be published this week, but I promise beloved, I was wiped out. So I spoke to a few friends and then called it a night. Even this day's journal, I'm doing it 2 days later! Yup, that's my confession.

1. Thank You GOD for loving me.
2. Thank You GOD for making me feel like royalty.
3. Thank You GOD for stellar treatment.
4. Thank You GOD for the finances to treat myself to a salon day every month.
5. Thank You GOD for making my nails beautiful.
6. Thank You GOD for teaching me how to simply praise You.
7. Thank You GOD for time management.
8. Thank You GOD for my parents and their health.

9. Thank You GOD for helping me get all I need done.

10. Thank You GOD for helping me publish this book and *Epistles to Abba* in time to have them shipped to me and sent to Jamaica.

11. Thank You GOD for divine connections.

12. Thank You GOD for another sale of our book, *Christianity 101: The ABC's and 123's of The Faith* and this time it's in North Carolina!

13. Thank You GOD for another divine connection with a bookstore in Jamaica.

14. Thank You GOD for allowing me to witness some of the things you've divinely orchestrated to move our books!

15. Thank You GOD.

Title: *Time:*   *Date:*

Your Day/Feelings/Thoughts/Prayer

"O magnify the Lord with me, And let us exalt His name together." – Psalm 34:3

Your day 26

How were you a blessing today? (A kind word or gesture you offered someone.)

What are you thankful for?

1. Thank You GOD
2. Thank You GOD
3. Thank You GOD
4. Thank You GOD
5. Thank You GOD

Your day 26

"O magnify the Lord with me, And let us exalt His name together." – Psalm 34:3

Day 27 ~ GOD's Greatest Blessings

~ 08.24.2020

It's the simple things we overlook that are some of GOD's greatest blessings.

I worked the overnight shift and had a pretty decent night. Things were steady which made the night go faster.

A colleague kept bugging me for my number. He'd been asking for months, and I've been saying no, but he literally hunted me down. He asked 3 people for me when he thought I left for the day. I was a little taken aback, but hey it is what it is. Wait, he even asked someone who doesn't know me at all where I was! He asked the housekeeping person! Anyhow, we ended up running into each other when suddenly everyone started telling me he was looking for me. He's married so he's off limits! I don't date married men, period! I know he has a ton of things he does which could be beneficial. He's an artist and a contractor, all things I could use. Anyhow, I left and went to 2 home improvement stores to pick out a few tiles for mom. While I was there, guess who called? You guessed it, my coworker. He said he called to say hi, but because my background was so loud, I struggled to hear him. I did manage to answer his question about what I was buying. I told him tile and he referred me to another place and said they have a huge selection way cheaper than the 2 locations I had on my list. I was so excited. Suddenly I realized, this is GOD giving me resources so I can save. Well, I didn't go to where he said because I was super tired, but I made a mental note and told mom. I went home and off to bed I went. I was so tired and believe it or not even as I type I am saying I really need to go to sleep. I'm pretty exhausted.

Beloved, never look at things as a coincidence. Always look at them for what they are, GOD-incidents. Blessings and love beloved.

1. Thank You GOD for loving me.

2. Thank You GOD for blessing me.

3. Thank You GOD for always standing by my side.

4. Thank You GOD for making me the apple of Your eye.

5. Thank You GOD for rest.

6. Thank You GOD for guidance.

7. Thank You GOD for letting me know I am truly blessed.

8. Thank You GOD for such wonderful blessings.

9. Thank You GOD for Your time invested in me.

10. Thank You GOD.

Title: Time: Date:

Your Day/ Feelings/ Thoughts/ Prayer

"...so that with one accord you may with one voice glorify the God and Father of our Lord Jesus Christ." – Romans 15:6

Your day 27

How were you a blessing today? (A kind word or gesture you offered someone.)

What are you thankful for?

1. Thank You GOD
2. Thank You GOD
3. Thank You GOD
4. Thank You GOD
5. Thank You GOD

Your day 27

"...so that with one accord you may with one voice glorify the God and Father of our Lord Jesus Christ."

– Romans 15:6

Day 28 ~ GOD-Incidents

~ 08.25.2020

No such thing as coincidences.

A dear friend happens to be on a 40 day fast during the time I'm doing the 30 days of gratitude. We spoke early this morning about things of GOD and how life becomes more doable when we give it all over to Him. Lo and behold, my friend informed me, today makes day 28 of 40 days of fasting! Now is this just a coincidence that both of us happen to be on day 28?! I think not. As I mentioned in the prior day's journal, there are no such things as coincidences. There are only GOD-incidents. I'm not sure of the significance of the 28th day or the number 28, but what I'll say is what came to mind when she said it. We both started a spiritual journey to better ourselves and become closer to GOD on the same day! Go figure.

I recall telling my friend that GOD has called me to give Him praises for the next 30 days and I know at that time she mentioned she was on a fast with the church. She's going through a rather trying time to the point I'd even equate her to the female version of Job. Well at least somewhat. We chatted it up this morning for about an hour and we arrived at this very question, if GOD says we have free will, why is it certain people sometimes are not allowed to execute their plans. Instead, they end up following the plans of GOD? Immediately, I heard the still voice of Holy Spirit say, "There are those who worship, love, and seek My face. They pray to Me asking for assistance. Then some do not. They don't believe in me." Suddenly, I knew exactly what the Father was saying. I got the story of Jonah in my mind. GOD commissioned Jonah to go warn the people of Nineveh of the impending wrath GOD would bring upon them, but Jonah wanted to let the people of Nineveh perish. GOD said no! Jonah considered the residents of Nineveh to be a stiffed neck people. Even as Jonah refused to carry the message of GOD to the people of Nineveh, GOD caused Jonah to be swallowed by a giant fish! Eventually when Jonah decided to do the will of the Father, he was then released from the belly of a giant fish. Now, one would say, where is Jonah's free will? He chose not to listen? Then because he chose not to listen, GOD threw him into the belly of a fish?! I hear you loud and clear beloved. Allow me to share the explanation I received from Holy Spirit. Let's start with scripture. Psalm 37:23 says, *"The steps of a good man are ordered by the LORD: and he delighteth in his way."* That's what I heard when we ran into our question. By the way, that happens to be one of my favorite scriptures. I digress. I completely understood what the Father was saying. In essence, when we pray to GOD, seek His face, and will, we are putting our faith in Him. We are saying GOD, we trust You and we're giving the Father the right to intervene in our life. As such, the Father steps in and does what He knows is necessary to get us on the right path. As it's evident Jonah had a relationship with GOD, the Father was able to step in and have His will be done for the people of Nineveh despite Jonah's stubbornness. The Father stepped in because He had a relationship with Jonah. As for those persons who choose a lack of intimacy with GOD, the Father will probably take the back seat in their life. The LORD may even give them over to a reprobate mind!

So beloved, the next time you begin wondering why GOD's doing as He pleases in your life, i.e.: not answering your prayers, be reminded you invited Him in. You've given Him the right to do what's in your best interest.

1. Thank You GOD for loving me.
2. Thank You GOD for blessing me.
3. Thank You GOD for always standing by my side.
4. Thank You GOD for wisdom.
5. Thank You GOD for revealing biblical truths to me.
6. Thank You GOD for always being there for me.
7. Thank You GOD for continuing to amaze me.
8. Thank You GOD for allowing your daughters to have fellowship.

9. Thank You GOD I never grow unimpressed with You.

10. Thank You GOD for putting a smile on my face.

11. Thank You GOD for guidance.

12. Thank You GOD You've taught me how to surrender.

13. Thank You GOD for a strategy to deal with the enemy.

14. Thank You GOD I'm not alone.

15. Thank You GOD for understanding me.

16. Thank You GOD I am Your absolute favorite!

17. Thank You GOD, You love me most!

18. Thank You GOD, I am the disciple whom Jesus loves!

Title: Time: Date:

Your Day/Feelings/Thoughts/Prayer

"Ascribe to the Lord the glory due His name; Bring an offering, and come before Him;
Worship the Lord in holy array." – 1 Chronicles 16:29

Your day 28

How were you a blessing today? (A kind word or gesture you offered someone.)

What are you thankful for?

1. Thank You GOD
2. Thank You GOD
3. Thank You GOD
4. Thank You GOD
5. Thank You GOD

Your day 28

"Ascribe to the Lord the glory due His name; Bring an offering, and come before Him; Worship the Lord in holy array." – 1 Chronicles 16:29

Day 29 ~ My Brother's Keeper

~ 08.26.2020

Emotional cleansing, is that what it's called?

Today started as my usual day. Well maybe not. I woke up, prayed, showered, and began my typing. *Epistles to Abba: Letters From the Heart* is what I was working on. As I started to complete the editing, I felt Holy Spirit nudge me to pray for a sister who suffered from several mini strokes. She's fairly young and dealing with recovering from the detrimental effects of the stroke. After praying for her, I was nudged again to pray for a very close friend who deals with occasional epileptic episodes and fibromyalgia. Both friends are extremely strong. Both are what us Christians call, 'giants in the faith." Both continue to minister the Word of GOD, intercede for others, and maintain a positive attitude. Trust me, these 2 women are nothing short of amazing!

The 2nd person I prayed for is more of a sister to me. She's been there throughout the years praying, uplifting, listening to my silliness, and simply being there to crack up with me. Anyone who truly knows me, knows I love to joke, and even more so, I love to laugh. Oddly enough, a male friend always starts laughing hysterically whenever he hears me laugh. He says I have a hearty deep-down sincere laugh. When I asked him what that means, he said, "Your laugh is sincere." Again, I digress. After I prayed and talked to my friend for some time, I went back to formatting *Epistles to Abba*. The next thing I know, a friend who's off to Scotland phoned me and we literally talked almost all day! It was an in-depth conversation where we went from point A to Z covering all topics. We talked: GOD, religion, politics, work-life, relationships – platonic and intimate, childhood experiences, family, health, and moving forward after devastations. We even briefly discussed finances! I knew I'd have to work super hard today because I ate up most of my time chatting with friends, but I wouldn't trade it for anything. Sincere relationships are hard to come by.

In the middle of our conversation, an old friend called, and I mean that both figuratively and literally. My friend Betty who just turned 96 this month called and said she hasn't forgotten about me! Listen, I have been calling her for over a year and haven't been able to get a hold of her. She was living independently until about 2 years ago when she took a fall. After the fall, her niece traveled from Texas to Florida to move her into a nursing home. Her niece always offered to relocate her to Texas, but Betty, being as stubborn as a mule, always declined. So off to the nursing home she went! Betty was adamant about these 2 things: 1- staying in her home and being independent and 2 – not leaving Florida. Well, she got 1 of the 2. She's still in Florida! You go, Betty! Each time I'd call, I'd get her answering machine, no Betty, and no returned phone call. I'd call her niece and she would say she's not sure what's happening because that's her contact information. Anyhow, Betty, bless her heart, spoke to me briefly and told me she's not allowed to leave her room due to COVID-19. She said they keep them in their rooms. Then she told me she is having extensive rehabilitation, but I couldn't hear why. I tell you this, Betty might be very hard of hearing, but she definitely is one of the sharpest tools in the shed! She gave me her phone number and her new address, even down to the apartment number!!! I had all her information because her niece gave it to me, but the mere fact that at 96 she can recite a new address is outstanding! We ended the call and suddenly my heart sunk. I was so very sad thinking about her and how she mentioned they took her car away from her. Betty golfed and drove everywhere well into her 90's! Oh and no, she wasn't driving crazily, she drove like a pro.

I called my friend who's relocating to Scotland because I had her on hold until eventually, she hung up. As I was telling her about Betty what do you know, all the tears started streaming down my face. I couldn't get a hold of myself! It was so sad to hear Betty being kept in her room, without her regular social life, no car, no golfing, and the like. It saddened me to hear that she could barely hear what I was saying no matter how much I yelled. I think the reality of her possibly going home soon to the Father, pretty much hit me. So there I was, crying like a baby on the phone with my friend. My friend felt the hurt and just tried soothing me, but later said, "Sometimes we just need a good cry. Sophia, you are a very strong person. Going through all you face at work and then all the other things you have to deal with, I mean it, you are sooo strong." I told her it's all GOD, it's not me.

You know beloved, you never know what someone is going through. I believe everyone should make it their business to talk with others and show they care about what they are going through. So many people face grave situations. Most of the time people on the outside don't have a clue what's going on.

Beloved, you're not an ostrich! Stop hiding your head in the sand! Become like an eagle. Fly high and cultivate a sharp eye. Maintain the ability to soar high and don't become trapped in toxic situations. Or like the Ryukin, the Japanese manufactured goldfish with translucent scales and skin, making evident a visibly beating heart and mind! Or like the transparent Ikakogi glass frog, the newly discovered species endemic to the isolated mountain area of Northern Columbia. It lives in the isolated Sierra Nevada de Santa Marta region and is fully transparent. Forgive me for giving a lesson in taxonomy!

Brethren, be careful. Guard your heart and mind, but don't become callous! Remember, you *are* your brother's keeper.

"Bear ye one another's burdens, and so fulfil the law of Christ." Galatians 6:2.

1. Thank You GOD for a heart filled with compassion.
2. Thank You GOD for helping me take Your commandments seriously.
3. Thank You GOD for blessing me.
4. Thank You GOD You've made me trustworthy.
5. Thank You GOD for wisdom.
6. Thank You GOD for making me take on my sister's burden.

7. Thank You GOD for how You've made me.

8. Thank You GOD I can be there for others.

9. Thank You GOD for You have blessed me.

10. Thank You GOD for loving me.

11. Thank You GOD for always standing by my side.

Your day 29

Title: Time: Date:

Your Day/Feelings/Thoughts/Prayer

"Whether, then, you eat or drink or whatever you do, do all to the glory of God."

– 1 Corinthians 10:31

Your day 29

How were you a blessing today? (A kind word or gesture you offered someone.)

What are you thankful for?

1. Thank You GOD
2. Thank You GOD
3. Thank You GOD
4. Thank You GOD
5. Thank You GOD

Your day 29

Day 30 ~ When GOD Does The Miraculous

~ 08.27.2020

Sow and you'll grow.

While trying to complete *Epistles to Abba: Letters From the Heart*, I got a phone call from a friend asking for prayer. She's currently in the midst of a storm dealing with losing her home of more than 15 years. It's always a pleasure to pray for someone, especially those I have a friendship with. I've noticed when you take the focus off yourself and redirect your energy to helping others, your world seems to become so much better. Several things happen when you put others first. One, you're able to begin putting things in proper perspective, often times realizing your issues are really not issues. Two, the blessings you receive – satisfaction knowing you helped someone else despite your situation is always a plus. Finally, number 3, which is most important, you are doing the will of GOD! By showing love, compassion, and by sharing in your brother's burden(s), you *are* doing GOD's will. What a tremendous blessing it is to know you are pleasing the Father by taking the focus off yourself. This is an example of selflessness.

So with the request, I paused, and I prayed. The very prayer request I prayed, was answered the same day! I was floored! Not because I wondered if GOD *would* do it, but because I never lose the zeal of excitement when GOD does the miraculous!

I'm thanking GOD He continues to answer prayers. I'm thanking GOD for His faithfulness.

1. Thank You GOD for You are faithful.
2. Thank You GOD for answered prayers.
3. Thank You GOD You helped me make it through my 30 days.
4. Thank You GOD for always standing by my side.

5. Thank You GOD You continue to speak to me.

6. Thank You GOD for Your love for me.

7. Thank You GOD for the words You give me to speak.

8. Thank You GOD for allowing me to write so freely.

9. Thank You GOD there's no burden on me.

10. Thank You GOD for making me, me!

Your day 30

Title: Time: Date:

Your Day/Feelings/Thoughts/Prayer

"For I was an hungred, and ye gave me meat: I was thirsty, and ye gave me drink: I was a stranger, and ye took me in:…" – Matthew 25:35

Your day 30

How were you a blessing today? (A kind word or gesture you offered someone.)

What are you thankful for?

1. Thank You GOD
2. Thank You GOD
3. Thank You GOD
4. Thank You GOD
5. Thank You GOD

Your day 30

"For I was an hungred, and ye gave me meat: I was thirsty, and ye gave me drink: I was a stranger, and ye took me in:..." – Matthew 25:35

206

Day 31 ~ Job Well Done! Your Final Thoughts

~ 08.28.2020

Temptations, pitfalls, setbacks, and lessons learned. This promotes growth!

Question, am I being disobedient by having a 31st day? Hum, I don't think so. Here's why. Day 31 is the final journaling exercise. Can you believe it, you've managed to accomplish getting 30 days under your belt! Day 31 is the day reserved for reflection. Yes, today is the day you set aside to reflect on your month, your *30 Days of Gratitude*. Use today to revisit your entire month of writing and start reflecting. If you don't feel like reading the entire day's journal, an easy way to go about things is to look at your day's title and subtitle (the 1st sentence after the day's title) if you included one. This will help jog your memory. Summarize your month of giving gratitude to GOD. Use *this* day to write down your lessons learned during the month and take your time. Note your growth, any temptations, pitfalls, and/or setbacks you encountered.

During my 30 days, one major temptation and pitfall I faced was asking GOD for things. Although this didn't happen often, I found myself asking GOD for things like, safe travels for friends. I also caught myself preparing to ask GOD how much to charge for this book?! Yeah, you're probably saying, really Sophia?! Yes, really. I know it *seems* simple, but it does fall under *asking* for something. That was really difficult for me. Thank GOD, I caught myself and sought wise counsel. I did have a few times I asked the Father for something and then had to immediately turn it around! So, no beloved, I didn't hit the mark 100%, but I thank GOD for His mercy, grace, and forgiveness. GOD knows our hearts and for that, I am *so* grateful.

Lesson learned 1: On the 25th as I finished journaling for the day and was sitting just having random thoughts, Holy Spirit whispered this my spirit, "This is why I wanted you to start the 30 Days of Gratitude sooner than you did." What does that mean, you're wondering? It means, had I started journaling when I *first* heard the Father tell me to, not exactly sure when that was, but I'd say maybe a week or 2 before I actually started, I wouldn't be rushing to get everything done. Dad is going to Jamaica on business, and I'm sending a few books with him for the bookstore. Initially, I thought, it was only supposed to be *Christianity 101: The ABC's and 123's of The Faith*, but later I found out it was supposed to be all 3 books! This would include *Epistles to Abba: Letters From the Heart* and *this* very book, *30 Days of Gratitude: Use Your Words to Change Your Life*. If I would've started sooner, I would've had more than enough time to get everything out before September 13th! Lesson learned!

22 "And Samuel said, Hath the LORD as great delight in burnt offerings and sacrifices, as in obeying the voice of the LORD? Behold, to obey is better than sacrifice, and to hearken than the fat of rams. 23 For rebellion is as the sin of witchcraft, and stubbornness is as iniquity and idolatry." ~ <u>1 Samuel 15:22-23</u>

7 "Be not deceived; God is not mocked: for whatsoever a man soweth, that shall he also reap. 8 For he that soweth to his flesh shall of the flesh reap corruption; but he that soweth to the Spirit shall of the Spirit reap life everlasting. 9 And let us not be weary in well doing: for in due season we shall reap, if we faint not. 10 As we have therefore opportunity, let us do good unto all men, especially unto them who are of the household of faith." ~ <u>Galatians 6:7-10</u>. I digress.

<u>Lesson learned 2</u>: Here's what is resonates in my spirit, the prayers of the righteous avails much. I used to say that all the time, but then stopped. The Father reminded me that I *am* righteous. So, I say this to you, you never have to wonder if you're doing right by GOD. Well maybe I should say, one way to tell if you are doing right by GOD is to perform a test. Pray for others and wait on their testimony of answered prayer. When you hear that, you know GOD is pleased because the prayers of the righteous avails much. Like when I prayed for a friend and the prayer was answered immediately. That's just my quick way of performing a self check.

Lesson learned 3: I don't have to ask the Father for anything. All I have to do is thank Him for everything! Yes, the bible says *ask and it shall be given unto you* and of course, if it's in the Word, then it's the infallible truth. Certainly, there is nothing wrong with asking, however, you don't have to ask when you can express gratitude. Just stand on faith. Gratitude *is* the highest form of praise. I believe this is the biggest lesson I learned. I've learned I can pray to the Father thanking Him in advance for everything I have, had, I am destined to have. It's a way to express my desires. Even with doing so, this teaches you to trust GOD. This is a faith-building exercise. When you stand praying to the Father and thanking Him for what you "have" (believing for a supernatural manifestation) you start believing you will receive that very thing you are praying for.

I've found that giving gratitude is a truly refreshing act. There's no pressure. You're simply thanking the Father for the very things He has done, is doing, and will do. It moves you from an area of complaint and ungratefulness to an area pleasing to the Father, gratitude and contentment. It's liberating not having to worry about I need this, I need that, and all the things we worry about. Instead, you thank GOD for what you already have and by doing so, it highlights how truly blessed you are. I'll admit, I slipped up a bit and started asking GOD during prayers, but the gentle sweet nudge of Holy Spirit reminded me not to ask. How kind.

When friends called requesting prayer, I informed them I cannot ask, but I will pray. My prayers for them were just as those for myself. I thanked GOD for the very thing they were requesting and left it there.

Lesson learned 4: Extreme spiritual warfare. During my 30 days of gratitude, I experienced the heights of spiritual warfare! When I tell you there was drama coming from every angle, I mean it! I had people attacking me over nothing! I had major difficulties trying to get my 2nd book done, which as a matter of fact as I type, it's still unfinished! I've been having formatting issues for about a whole week and just as I decided to publish the book with the minor errors, the platform I use spat out an error message stating their system is down! REALLY!!?? I snapped a picture of the error message and sent it to 3 friends plus mom. Not that they wouldn't believe me, but occasionally, it's nice to show proof.

So, is GOD stretching me? Yes, indeed He absolutely is! I feel pushed *and* stretched, but I'm thankful to GOD for it. There's no greater coach than the Father. There's no greater advisor than the Father. There's no greater being than GOD!

During the past 30 days of giving gratitude, I felt at peace. Although it's been a tumultuous ride, it was all worth it. I had people call themselves *telling me about myself* while saying they are coming in the name of Jesus and with the love of the LORD. Seriously? You can't make this stuff up! I've had people tell me; I care too much. Huh? Well, if that's not a bleep, I don't know what is. Can someone ever really care too much? Thank GOD for the Spirit of the LORD, Holy Spirit who whispered to me, "It's called a spirit of excellence." Ahhh-mazing! That made me feel better!

In a world overflowing with darkness and wickedness, it is refreshing to know that my caring equates to a spirit of excellence. The bible does say there will be a time where people call good evil and evil good. Do you suppose that's what that was because we're definitely in a time where this is happening? I used to be accused of that very thing often and it slowed down. It was nice to hear it again because it alerts me to the character I exude. Thank You GOD for a spirit of excellence. Thank You GOD for such revelation.

During the past 30 days, I've had people lie on me and turn an entire group of people against me. My car started acting crazy and with all the fixes, I still have more tweaking to get done. I've had major spiritual warfare come against me with the writing of book #2 and this one, book #3. One of my closest friends became quite ill and the list goes on. No need to rehash or provide a laundry list of oppositions, but I felt the need to give you a brief insight to my monthly events. Seriously, it has been so trying and a bit much. I had one friend say he's never seen such level of attack. The layers of continuous blockage are unreal. He also said it's almost like one would think I am making up all the things happening to me. Then he said, "Seriously, it kind of makes me want to pull away from you because I don't want anything trickling down to me." Wow! Now there's a statement for you! I appreciate his honesty. Shortly after saying that, he then said, "But I know better," and I understood. Earlier that day in the wee hours of the morning he told me I am like Jonah! Huh?! I was baffled because I know I am not disobeying GOD. He explained, it's like several people's lives being jeopardized because of one individual with a call from GOD. He said all that based on an incident I encountered at work. So again, not to wave my endless list of opposition in your face, I simply want to assure you get a crystal-clear picture of the type of month I had.

Another friend said, "People think giving GOD gratitude for 30 days is going to be a walk in the park. No, not so! There's going to be a lot of spiritual warfare happening."

During this time of gratitude, GOD made things plain. He spoke to me by confirming the 30 days of gratitude walk with run-ins of gratitude topics in one book I was reading and the other book in my presence. The Father also paralleled my gratitude time with a friend on a 40 day fast. Unbeknownst to us, we both started our journey together and when I hit the 30-day mark, the Father had her announce it was her 30th day of fasting!

By now I hope I've embedded it into your mind that there is no such thing as a coincidence. I assure you, there are only GOD-incidents! During my 30 days of gratitude, one fact has definitely been solidified in my mind, and that is, GOD *will* have His way!

Abundant blessings and love.

Sophia

Your month, day 31

Title: Time: Date:

Your Day/Feelings/Thoughts/Prayer

"I know both how to be abased, and I know how to abound: everywhere and in all things I am instructed both to be full and to be hungry, both to abound and to suffer need." – Philippians 4:12

Your month, day 31

How were you a blessing overall? (Think of the kind words & gestures you offered over the course of the past 30 days.)

What are you most thankful for?

1. Thank You GOD
2. Thank You GOD
3. Thank You GOD
4. Thank You GOD
5. Thank You GOD

Your month, day 31

Your month, day 31

"I know both how to be abased, and I know how to abound: everywhere and in all things I am instructed both to be full and to be hungry, both to abound and to suffer need." – Philippians 4:12

Take a sabbatical from asking GOD for things.

~ Dr. Sophia Mattis ~

Afterword

30 Days of Gratitude Use your words to change your life is the foundational book in the series. It was birthed when I heard the LORD say, "No more asking for things. For the next 30 days don't ask for anything." My instructions were simple, 1. Don't ask God for anything for the next 30 days, 2. Journal each day during that timeframe, 3. Put it all in a book, and 4. Make it a workbook so others can do the same.

What started out as my personal journey has morphed into an entire global movement. 30 Days of Gratitude has people from all over the world come together quarterly to participate in a months long session of taking a sabbatical from asking GOD for things. The movement entails community support by way of daily scriptures plus positive affirmations, prayers, and weekly – Don't be shy, Testify – testimonials sessions. I have included all parts used during the movement in separate books. This 3-part package is intended for those who wish to continue journeying upon completing our live sessions and newcomers wishing to experience the journey. This opportunity allows you to experience the benefits of the 30-day journey in between the quarterly sessions.

For a real-life experience with other journeyers, you can join in during one of our live sessions offered during one or all the seasons – winter, spring, summer, fall. Contact me at asksophiebella3@gmail.com and I'll add you to the journeyer's list. Hope to see you there!

Journey Package Includes:

1. 30 Days of Gratitude (Prayer companion)

2. 30 Days of Gratitude (One [1] Seasonal Edition journal)

3. 30 Days of Gratitude (Scripture plus positive affirmations)

Books by the Author

CURRENT

Christianity 101: The ABC's and 123's of The Faith

Epistles to Abba: Letters from the Heart

Our Father's Pot Daily Journal Plus Affirmations

30 Days of Gratitude: Use Your Words to Change Your Life*

UPCOMING

30 Days of Gratitude: Use Your Words to Change Your Life – Prayer Companion

30 Days of Gratitude: Use Your Words to Change Your Life – Rest, Refresh, Refocus 30 Day Journey Companion

30 Days of Gratitude: Use Your Words to Change Your Life – Winter Edition

30 Days of Gratitude: Use Your Words to Change Your Life – Spring Edition

30 Days of Gratitude: Use Your Words to Change Your Life – Summer Edition

30 Days of Gratitude: Use Your Words to Change Your Life – Fall Edition

30 Days of Gratitude: Use Your Words to Change Your Life – All Seasons Journal

Christianity 101: The ABC's and 123's of The Faith Study Guide

In the Beginning: Genesis Reviewed

In the Beginning: Genesis Reviewed Study Guide

TOL – Thinking Out Loud: A Weekly Meditation

About the Author

Serving as an interim radio co-host, guest minister/speaker at multiple venues, Dr. SOPHIA MATTIS' voice has been heard worldwide. She is a devout Christian born in Jamaica West Indies. As a physician, motivational speaker, author, and lecturer residing in Long Island, New York, holding degrees in Medicine, Health Services Administration, and Sociology it's evident Sophia is passionate about the well-being of mankind. She is focused and determined to heal the minds of GOD's children by way of His Word. Dr. Mattis' love for GOD nourishes her mission to heal the mind of the destitute. She focuses her attention heavily on disadvantaged children, the elderly, and the homeless. Dr. Mattis hopes to usher in the *Light* of GOD into the dark places in the minds of those she encounters while winning numerous souls for GOD's Kingdom by preaching the gospel and professing the name of Jesus Christ of Nazareth.

Throughout the years, Dr. Mattis has written numerous health and wellness newspaper articles while providing weekly encouraging segments for various online Christian newspapers. Currently, Dr. Mattis has published *Christianity 101: The ABC's, Epistles to Abba: Letters from the Heart,* and *123's of The Faith* and *Our Father's Pot Daily Journal Plus Affirmations*. She has several Christian books pending publication.

Spearheading events such as: the United Nation's International Day of Peace – (an initiative focusing on combat gang violence within her community), N.A.C.I. – Never Alone Care Initiative – an initiative providing toiletries to the less fortunate), and OFP – Our Father's Pot – (a monthly gathering where women discuss pressing matters), are some of the undertakings she engages. To help combat hunger and homelessness on Long Island, Dr. Mattis helps distribute food both at her local church and soup kitchen. Dr. Mattis is an active *Biometrics Medical Review Board Member* who continuously seeks out volunteering opportunities during her travels, to assist in enhancing dilapidated communities and feeding those who are less fortunate.

Dr. Mattis' love for GOD, His people, evangelism, healing, teaching, and philanthropy, motivates her to minister the Word of GOD worldwide. She attributes her knowledge of the Word to the Holy Spirit's teaching and leading.

Contact the Author:

Email: asksophiebella3@gmail.com

Write to: Sophia Mattis, MD, MHSA

209 Glen Cove Rd.

Suite 508

Carle Place, N.Y. 11514

Index

Salvation Prayer

To be saved, it is as simple as confessing and believe what the Word of GOD says in **Romans 10:9**:

"If thou shalt confess with thy mouth the LORD Jesus and believe in your heart that GOD has raised Him from the dead, thou shalt be saved."

Do you believe what you just read? If so, you *have now* been saved!

The prayer below is not necessary; it is for those who wish to pray a bit more.

I confess with my mouth and believe in my heart that "Jesus is LORD" and Savior of my life. I believe in my heart that GOD raised Jesus Christ of Nazareth from the dead. The bible says Jesus is the way, the truth, and the life and because I want life eternal with the Holy Father, Abba, I have confessed, believe, and now I repent of all my sins so I may be saved. I believe and am justified by my heart, and I am saved by the confession of my mouth. Amen.

www.ingramcontent.com/pod-product-compliance
Lightning Source LLC
Chambersburg PA
CBHW080541090426

42734CB00016B/3174